MW00749181

SMALL TALK

Northern Europe

10
ESSENTIAL
LANGUAGES
FOR
CITY BREAKS

Small Talk Northern Europe
1st edition – March 2008

Published by
Lonely Planet Publications Pty Ltd ABN 36 005 607 983
90 Maribyrnong St, Footscray, Victoria 3011, Australia

Lonely Planet Offices
Australia Locked Bag 1, Footscray, Victoria 3011
USA 150 Linden St, Oakland CA 94607
UK 2nd Floor, 186 City Rd, London, EC1V 2NT

Commissioning Editor Karin Vidstrup Monk **Series Designer** Yukiyoshi Kamimura **Editor** Branislava Vladisavljevic **Layout Designer** David Kemp **Cartographer** Wayne Murphy **Text Contributor** Jodie Martire

Authors Adam Hyllestad, Emma Koch, Per Langgård, John Mitchinson, Karin Vidstrup Monk, Eliza Reid, Rytis Radavicius, Uno Schultz, Anne Stensletten, Päivi Tuomisto, Livija Varna-Uskalis

Cover Girl taking photos, Bruce Bi/Lonely Planet Images; People watching sunset, Izzet Keribar/Lonely Planet Images; Tree in the winter snow, David Tipling/Lonely Planet Images

ISBN 978 1 74179 240 9

text © Lonely Planet Publications Pty Ltd 2008
images © Lonely Planet Images 2008
(unless otherwise noted on page 127)

10 9 8 7 6 5 4 3 2

Printed by Hang Tai Printing Company, China

At a glance	5
Map	6
Festivals	8
Public holidays	12

Danish 13

Estonian 23

Faroese 33

Finnish 43

Greenlandic 53

Contents

Icelandic 63

Latvian 73

Lithuanian 83

Norwegian 93

Swedish 103

24 hours in the city 113

Index 124

Northern Europe – at a glance

Going away for the day, the weekend or the classic short break? *Small Talk Northern Europe* gives you the essential language you need to live it up in Northern Europe. Get hot tips in our '24 hours in the city' feature and talk your way to the coldest draught beer in Copenhagen, the best coffee and cake in Tallinn or the steamiest sauna in Helsinki. Dip into our 'Festivals' feature, get your party shoes on and take part in this exciting region's sizzling cultural life.

A bit about the languages ... Luckily, they all use Roman script, albeit with quirky added accents. The Scandinavian languages (Danish, Faroese, Icelandic, Norwegian and Swedish) are rooted in Old Norse, while Lithuanian and Latvian belong to the Baltic branch of the Indo-European language family. Finnish, known as *suomi* to the locals, is part of the exclusive Finno-Ugric language family, of which Estonian and Hungarian are the only other members. The 40,000 Greenlandic natives call their mother tongue (which belongs to the Eskimo-Aleut group of languages) *kalaallisut*. Whichever language – this is one region sure to set the senses in overdrive.

did you know?

- The only truly Scandinavian nations are Sweden, Norway and Denmark. Neighbouring Finland, Iceland and the Faroe Islands are often included in the Scandinavian club for geographical convenience, but to make sure no one gets offended use the kit-and-caboodle term 'the Nordic countries'.
- After Australia, Greenland is the world's largest island and it also contains the world's largest national park – the Northeast Greenland National Park, established in 1974.
- In 1989, over two million people joined hands to form The Baltic Way, a 600-kilometre line that stretched through Latvia, Estonia and Lithuania, to demand independence from the then-USSR. All three countries later achieved this aim.

abbreviations

f	feminine	sg	singular	inf	informal
m	masculine	pl	plural	pol	polite

Northern Europe

Greenland & Iceland

Qaanaaq (Thule)

Baffin Bay

**GREENLAND
(Denmark)**

Upernavik

Uummannaq

Qeqertarsuaq Ilulissat

Ittoqqortoormiit

*Davis
Strait* Sisimiut

Tasiilaq
(Ammassalik) *Denmark Strait* Akureyri

**Nuuk ⊙
(Godthåb)** **Reykjavík ✪ ICELAND**

*ATLANTIC
OCEAN*

Labrador Sea Qaqortoq

Canada

*NORWE
SE*

⊙ **Tórshavn
Faroe
Islands
(Denmark)**

0   500 km
0   300 mi

Kristiansund
Molde Trondheim
Ålesund

NORWAY

Lillehamn
Hama
Gjøvik

Bergen

Oslo ✪

Haugesund Skien Halc

Stavanger

Arendal

Kristiansand *Skagerrak*

Scotland *NORTH
SEA* Ålborg *Kat*

DENMARK
Herning Årh
Copen!

*United
Kingdom*

Esbjerg Kolding Oder

*Northern
Ireland*

Ireland *England* *German*

▨ Danish		▨ Greenlandic	
▨ Estonian		▨ Icelandic	
▨ Faroese		▨ Latvian	
▨ Finnish			

6

7

January

Mitaartut (festival similar to Halloween)	**Greenland**	6th
Tromsø International Film Festival	**Norway**	

February

Copenhagen International Fashion Fair	**Denmark**	
Fettisdagen (Mardi Gras)	**Sweden**	Shrove Tuesday
Jokkmokk Winter Market (Sami crafts & reindeer racing)	**Sweden**	
Kokkola Winter Accordion (music festival)	**Finland**	
Užgavėnės (carnival-type end of winter celebration)	**Lithuania**	seven weeks before Easter

March

Holmenkollen Ski Festival	**Norway**	
International Baltic Ballet Festival	**Latvia**	
Kaziuko Mugė (arts & crafts festival)	**Lithuania**	Sunday nearest to 4 March
Nuuk Snow Festival	**Greenland**	
Outdoor Winter Swimming Championship	**Finland**	
Sami Easter Festival	**Norway**	Mar/Apr
World Ice Golf Championship	**Greenland**	

April

Inferno Metal Festival (music festival)	**Norway**	
Jurgines (spring celebration of nature)	**Lithuania**	23rd
Sumardagurinn Fyrsti (First Day of Summer)	**Iceland**	third Thursday
Walpurgis Night (celebration of spring)	**Scandinavia & Nordic Europe**	30th

May

Riga International Fantasy Film Festival	**Latvia**	
Vappu (spring carnival)	**Finland**	1st

June

Jāņi (summer solstice celebration)	**Latvia**	23rd
Klaipeda Castle Jazz Festival	**Lithuania**	
Midsummer's Eve	**Scandinavia & Nordic Europe**	late Jun
Roskilde Festival (outdoor music festival)	**Denmark**	Jun/Jul
St Jonas' Festival (folk festival)	**Lithuania**	23rd
Sjómannadagurinn (seafarers' festival)	**Iceland**	
Skagen Music Festival	**Denmark**	
Summartónar (summer music festival held in various cities)	**Faroe Islands**	Jun/Jul
Tar-Burning Week (including tar rowing)	**Finland**	late Jun

July

Binding of the Wreaths Festival (lovers' festival)	**Lithuania**	20th
Copenhagen Jazz Festival	**Denmark**	
G! Festival (outdoor music festival)	**Faroe Islands**	
Laulupidu (Estonian Song Festival)	**Estonia**	every five years
Olai Festival (honouring St Olav, patron saint of the Faroese)	**Faroe Islands**	28th–30th
Rīgas Ritmi (music festival)	**Latvia**	
Savolinna Opera Festival	**Finland**	
Stockholm Pride Festival (gay community festival)	**Sweden**	Jul/Aug
Wife-Carrying World Championship	**Finland**	

August

Medeltidsveckan (Medieval Week)	**Sweden**
Mobile Phone Throwing World Championship	**Finland**
Notodden Blues Festival	**Norway**
Þjóðhátíð (independence festival)	**Iceland**
Street Theatre Festival	**Estonia**
World Sauna Championship	**Finland**

September

Air Guitar World Championship	Finland	
Århus Festival (arts & culture festival)	Denmark	
Nordisk Panorama (Five Cities Film Festival)	Iceland	
Reykjavík Film Festival	Iceland	

October

Airwaves Festival (new music festival)	Iceland	
Arena New Music Festival	Latvia	
Films from the South Festival	Norway	
Nubaigai (harvest festival)	Lithuania	5th
Vilnius Jazz Festival	Lithuania	

November

All Souls' Day	Lithuania	2nd
Black Nights Film Festival	Estonia	Nov/Dec
Stockholm International Film Festival	Sweden	
Tivoli's Christmas Markets	Denmark	Nov/Dec

December

Luciadagen (Santa Lucia – festival of lights)	Sweden	13th
St Thomas Christmas Market	Finland	
Winter Solstice Festival	Latvia	18th–22nd

Public holidays

New Year's Day	1 January
Epiphany (Finland, Greenland, Sweden)	6 January
Independence Day (Lithuania)	16 February
First Day of Summer (Iceland)	Thursday after 18 April
May (Labour) Day	1 May
Common Prayer Day (Denmark, Greenland)	fourth Friday after Easter
Ascension Day (Denmark, Faroe Islands, Finland, Greenland, Iceland, Norway, Sweden)	40 days after Easter
Whitsunday/Whitmonday (Denmark, Faroe Islands, Finland, Greenland, Iceland, Norway, Sweden)	eighth Sunday/ Monday after Easter
Constitution Day (Denmark, Faroe Islands)	5 June
Midsummer's Day (Estonia, Finland, Latvia, Sweden)	around 21 June
Ullortuneq (Greenland's National Day)	21 June
Victory Day (Estonia)	23 June
Ólavsøka (Faroe Islands' National Day)	28–29 July
Shop & Office Workers' Day (Iceland)	first Monday in August
All Saints' Day (Finland, Lithuania, Sweden)	October/November
Independence Day (Latvia)	18 November
Independence Day (Finland)	6 December
Christmas Eve (Denmark, Faroe Islands, Finland, Greenland, Iceland)	24 December
Christmas Day	25 December
New Year's Eve (Faroe Islands, Greenland, Iceland)	31 December

Pulbic holidays

Danish

In Denmark, every corner of the country is in on the party.

Pronunciation

Vowels		Consonants	
Symbol	**English sound**	**Symbol**	**English sound**
a	act	b	bed
aa	father	ch	cheat
ai	aisle	d	dog
aw	saw	dh	that
e	bet	f	fat
ee	see	g	go
eu	nurse	h	hat
ew	ee pronounced with rounded lips	j	joke
		k	kit
ey	as in 'bet', but longer	l	lot
		m	man
i	hit	n	not
o	pot	ng	ring
oh	note	p	pet
oo	soon	r	red (trilled)
ow	how	s	sun
oy	toy	sh	shot
		t	top
		v	very
		w	win
		y	yellow

The Danish pronunciation is given in purple after each word or phrase. Read these words as though you were reading English and you're sure to be understood. Each syllable is separated by a dot, and italics indicate that you need to put stress on that syllable, for example:

Undskyld. *awn*·skewl

essentials

Yes./No.	*Ja./Nej.*	ya/nai
Hello./Goodbye.	*Hej./Farvel.*	hai/faar-*vel*
Please.	*Vær så venlig.*	ver saw *ven*-lee
Thank you (very much).	*(Mange) Tak.*	(*mang*-e) taak
You're welcome.	*Selv tak.*	sel taak
Excuse me.	*Undskyld mig.*	*awn*-skewl mai
Sorry.	*Undskyld.*	*awn*-skewl

Do you speak English?
  Taler De/du engelsk? pol/inf   *ta*-la dee/doo *eng*-elsk

Do you understand?
  Forstår De/du? pol/inf   for-*stawr* dee/doo

I (don't) understand.
  Jeg forstår (ikke).   yai for-*stawr* (*i*-ke)

chatting

introductions

Mr	*Hr*	heyr
Mrs/Miss	*Fru/Frøken*	froo/*freu*-ken
How are you?	*Hvordan går det?*	vor-*dan* gawr dey
Fine, thanks.	*Godt, tak.*	got taak
What's your name?	*Hvad hedder De/du?* pol/inf	va *hey*-dha dee/doo
My name is ...	*Mit navn er ...*	mit nown ir ...
I'm pleased to meet you.	*Hyggeligt at møde Dem/dig.* pol/inf	*hew*-ge-leet at *meu*-dhe dem/dai

Here's my (email) address.
  Her er min (email) adresse.   heyr ir meen (*ee*-mayl) a-*draa*-se

What's your (email) address?
  Hvad er Deres/din (email) adresse? pol/inf   va ir *de*-res/deen (*ee*-mayl) a-*draa*-se

15

Here's my phone number.
Her er mit telefonnummer.   heyr ir meet tey·ley·*fohn*·naw·ma

What's your phone number?
Hvad er Deres/dit   va ir *de*·res/deet
telefonnummer? pol/inf   tey·ley·*fohn*·naw·ma

What's your occupation?
Hvad laver De/du? pol/inf   va *la*·va dee/doo

I'm a ...	*Jeg er ...*	yai ir ...
businessperson	*forretnings-drivende*	for·*rat*·nings·dree·ve·ne
student	*studerende*	stoo·*dey*·re·ne

Where are you from?
Hvor kommer De/du fra? pol/inf   vor *ko*·ma dee/doo fraa

I'm from (England).
Jeg er fra (England).   yai ir fraa (*eng*·lan)

Are you married?
Er De/du gift? pol/inf   ir dee/doo geeft

I'm married/single.
Jeg er gift/ugift.   yai ir geeft/*oo*·geeft

How old are you?
Hvor gammel er?   vor *gaa*·mel ir

I'm ... years old.
Jeg er ... år gammel.   yai ir ... awr *gaa*·mel

making conversation

What's the weather like?
Hvordan er vejret?   vor·*dan* ir *vey*·ret

It's cold.	*Det er koldt.*	dey ir kolt
It's hot.	*Det er varmt.*	dey ir vaarmt
It's raining.	*Det regner.*	dey *rain*·a
It's snowing.	*Det sner.*	dey sneyr

Do you live here?	*Bor De/du her?* pol/inf	bohr dee/doo heyr
Where are you going?	*Hvor skal De/du hen?* pol/inf	vor skal dee/doo hen
What are you doing?	*Hvad laver De/du?* pol/inf	va *la*·va dee/doo

16

invitations

Would you like	*Har De/du*	haar dee/doo
to go (for a) …?	*lyst til …?* pol/inf	lewst til …
dancing	*at tage ud*	at taa oodh
	og danse	o *dan*·se
drink	*en drink*	in drink
meal	*at tage ud*	at ta oodh
	og spise	o *spee*·se
out	*at gå ud*	at gaw oodh

Yes, I'd love to.
Ja, det vil jeg meget gerne.   ya dey vil yai *maa*·yet *gir*·ne

No, I'm afraid I can't.
Nej, det kan jeg desværre ikke.   nai dey kan yai dey·*sve*·re *i*·ke

I love it here!
Her er skønt!
heyr ir skeunt

What time will we meet?
Hvornår skal vi mødes?   vor·*nawr* skal vee *meu*·dhes

Where will we meet?
Hvor skal vi mødes?   vor skal vee *meu*·dhes

Let's meet at …	*Lad os modes …*	ladh os *meu*·dhes …
(eight) o'clock	*klokken (otte)*	*klo*·ken (*aw*·te)
the entrance	*ved indgangen*	vi *in*·gaang·en

meeting up

Can I …?	*Må jeg …?*	maw yai …
dance with you	*danse med dig*	*dan*·se me dai
sit here	*sidde her*	*si*·dha heyr
take you home	*tage med dig hjem*	ta me dai jem

I'm here with my girlfriend/boyfriend.
Jeg er her med min kæreste.   yai ir heyr me meen *ker*·ste

It's been great meeting you.
Det har været fantastisk — dey haar *ve*·ret fan·*tas*·teesk
at møde Dem/dig. pol/inf — at *meu*·dhe dem/dai

Keep in touch!
Skriv til mig! — skreev til mai

likes & dislikes

I thought it was ...	*Jeg synes det var ...*	yai sewns dey vaar ...
It's ...	*Det er ...*	dey ir ...
awful	*hæsligt*	*hes*·leet
great	*fantastisk*	fan·*tas*·teesk
interesting	*interessant*	in·traa·*sant*
Do you like ...?	*Kan De/du*	kan dee/doo
	lide ...? pol/inf	lee ...
I (don't) like ...	*Jeg synes (ikke)*	yai sewns (*i*·ke)
	om ...	om ...
art	*kunst*	kawnst
shopping	*at handle*	at *han*·le
sport	*sport*	sport

eating & drinking

I'd like ..., please.	*Jeg vil gerne ..., tak.*	yai vil *gir*·ne ... taak
the nonsmoking section	*sidde i ikke-rygerafdelingen*	*si*·dha ee *i*·ke·rew·a·ow·*dey*·ling·en
the smoking section	*sidde i rygerafdelingen*	*si*·dha ee rew·a·ow·*dey*·ling·en
a table for (four)	*have et bord til (fire)*	ha it bohr til (feer)

Do you have vegetarian food?
Har I vegetarmad? — haar ee vey·ge·*taar*·madh

What would you recommend?
Hvad kan De/du anbefale? pol/inf — va kan dee/doo *an*·bey·fa·le

I'll have a ...	*..., tak.*	... taak
Cheers!	*Skål!*	skawl

I'd like (the) ..., please.	Jeg vil gerne have ...	yai vil gir·ne ha ...
bill	regningen	rai·ning·en
drink list	vinkortet	veen·kor·tet
menu	menuen	me·new·en
that dish	den ret	den ret

Would you like a drink?
Vil du have en drink?
vil doo haa in drink

(cup of) coffee/tea	(en kop) kaffe/te	(in kop) ka·fe/tey
(mineral) water	(mineral) vand	(mee·ne·ral) van
bottle of (beer)	en flaske (øl)	in flas·ke (eul)
glass of (wine)	et glas (vin)	it glas (veen)
breakfast	morgenmad	morn·madh
lunch	frokost	froh·kost
dinner	middag	mi·da

exploring

Where's the ...?	Hvor er der ...?	vor ir deyr ...
bank	en bank	in baank
hotel	et hotel	it hoh·tel
post office	et postkontor	it post·kon·tohr

Can you show me (on the map)?
Kan De/du vise mig det kan dee/doo vee·se mai dey
(på kortet)? pol/inf (paw kor·tet)

What time does it open/close?
Hvornår åbner/lukker de? vor·nawr awb·na/law·ka dey

What's the admission charge?
Hvad koster adgang? va kos·ta adh·gaang

When's the next tour?
Hvornår er den næste tur? vor·nawr ir den nes·te toor

Where can I find ...?	Hvor kan jeg finde ...?	vor kan yai fi·ne ...
clubs	natklubber	nat·kloo·ba
gay venues	bøsseklubber	beu·se·kloo·ba
pubs	pubber	paw·ba

Can we get there by public transport?

Kan vi tage offentlig transport dertil? kan vee ta o·fen·lee traans·port deyr·til

Where can I buy a ticket?

Hvor kan jeg købe en billet? vor ka yai keu·be in bi·let

One ... ticket (to Odense), please.	En ... billet (til Odense), tak.	in ... bee·let (til oh·dhen·se) taak.
one-way	enkelt	eng·kelt
return	retur	rey·toor

My luggage has been ...	Min bagage er blevet ...	meen ba·gaa·she ir bley·vet ...
lost	væk	vek
stolen	stjålet	styaw·let

Is this the ... to (Aarhus)?	Er dette ... til (Århus)?	ir dey·te ... til (awr·hoos)
boat	båden	baw·dhen
bus	bussen	boo·sen
plane	flyet	flew·et
train	toget	taw·et

What time's the ... bus?	Hvad tid er den ... bus?	va teedh ir den ... boos
first	første	feurs·te
next	næste	nes·te
last	sidste	sees·te

I'd like a taxi ...	Jeg vil gerne have en taxa ...	yai vil gir·ne ha in tak·sa ...
at (9am)	klokken (ni om morgenen)	klo·ken (nee om mor·nen)
tomorrow	i morgen	ee morn

How much is it to ...?

Hvad koster det at køre til ...? va kos·ta dey at keu·re til ...

Please take me to (this address).
Vær venlig at køre   ver *ven*·lee at *keu*·re
mig til (denne adresse).   mai til (*de*·ne a·*draa*·se)

Please stop here.
Venligst stop her.   *ven*·leest stop heyr

shopping

Where's the (market)?	*Hvor er der (et marked)?*	vor ir deyr (it *maar*·kedh)
I'm looking for ...	*Jeg leder efter ...*	yai *li*·dha ef·ta ...
It's faulty.	*Det er i stykker.*	dey ir ee *stew*·ka
I'd like ..., please.	*Jeg vil gerne have ..., tak.*	yai vil *gir*·ne ha ... taak
a refund	*en efundering*	in re·fawn·*dey*·ring
to return this	*returnere dette*	rey·toor·*ney*·re *dey*·te

How much is it?
Hvor meget koster det?   vor *maa*·yet *kos*·ta dey

Can you write down the price?
Kan De/du skrive   ka dee/doo *skree*·ve
prisen ned? pol/inf   *pree*·sen nidh

That's too expensive.
Det er for dyrt.   dey ir for dewrt

There's a mistake in the bill.
Der er en fejl i kvitteringen.   deyr ir in fail ee kvee·*tey*·ring·en

I need a film for this camera.
Jeg har brug for film   yai haar broo for feelm
til dette kamera.   til *dey*·te *ka*·me·raa

Do you accept ...?	*Tager I ...?*	ta ee ...
credit cards	*kreditkort*	kre·*deet*·kort
travellers cheques	*rejsechecks*	*rai*·se·sheks
I'd like ..., please.	*Jeg vil gerne have ..., tak.*	yai vil *gir*·ne ha ... taak
a receipt	*en kvittering*	in kvee·*tey*·ring
my change	*mine byttepenge*	*mee*·ne *bew*·te·peng·e

working

Where's the business centre?
Hvor er forretningscenteret?   vor ir for·*ret*·nings·sen·tredh

I'm attending a ...   *Jeg er ...*   yai ir ...
    conference   *til konference*   til kon·fe·*rang*·se
    course   *på kursus*   paw *koor*·soos
    meeting   *til møde*   til *meu*·dhe

I'm visiting a trade fair.
Jeg er til handelsmesse.   yai ir til *han*·els·me·se

I have an appointment with ...
Jeg har en aftale med ...   yai haar in *ow*·ta·la me ...

I'm with my colleagues.
Jeg er her med mine kolleger.   yai ir heyr me *mee*·ne koh·*ley*·a

Here's my business card.
Her er mit kort.   heyr ir meet kort

That went very well.
Det gik rigtigt godt.   det geek *rig*·tee got

emergencies

Help!	*Hjælp!*	yelp
Stop!	*Stop!*	stop
Go away!	*Gå væk!*	gaw vek
Thief!	*Tyv!*	tew
Fire!	*Ildebrand!*	ee·le·braan

Call ...!   *Ring efter ...!*   ring *ef*·ta ...
    an ambulance   *en ambulance*   in aam·boo·*laang*·se
    a doctor   *en læge*   in *le*·ye
    the police   *politiet*   poh·lee·*tee*·et

Could you help me, please?   *Kan De/du hjælpe mig?* pol/inf   kan dee/doo *yel*·pe mai

I'm lost.   *Jeg er faret vild.*   yai ir *faa*·ret veel

Where's the toilet?   *Hvor er toilettet?*   vor ir toy·*le*·tet

Estonian

Estonia – where the vowel sounds are deep, the food is rich and the experiences are unique.

Pronunciation

Vowels		Consonants	
Symbol	English sound	Symbol	English sound
a	run	b	bed
aa	father	ch	cheat
ai	aisle	d	dog
air	fair	f	fat
aw	law	g	go
ay	say	h	hat
e	bet	k	kit
ea	ear	kh	as the 'ch' in the Scottish loch
ee	see		
eu	nurse	l	lot
ew	ee pronounced with rounded lips	m	man
		n	not
ey	as in 'bet', but longer	p	pet
		r	red (trilled)
i	hit	s	sun
o	pot	sh	shot
oh	note	t	top
oo	zoo	ts	hats
ow	now	v	very
oy	toy	y	yellow
u	put	z	zero
uh	ago	zh	pleasure

The Estonian pronunciation is given in purple after each word or phrase. Read these words as though you were reading English and you're sure to be understood. Each syllable is separated by a dot, and italics indicate that you need to put stress on that syllable, for example: *Palun.* *pa*-lun

Estonian

essentials

Yes./No.	*Jaa./Ei.*	yaa/ay
Hello./Goodbye.	*Tere./Nägemist.*	te·re/nair·ge·mist
Please.	*Palun.*	pa·lun
Thank you (very much).	*Tänan (väga).*	tair·nan (vair·ga)
You're welcome.	*Palun.*	pa·lun
Excuse me.	*Vabandage.* pol	va·ban·da·ge
	Vabanda. inf	va·ban·da
Sorry.	*Vabandust.*	va·ban·dust

Do you speak English?
   Kas te räägite inglise keelt?   kas te rair·git·te ing·kli·se keylt

Do you understand?
   Kas te saate aru?   kas te saat·te a·ru

I understand.
   Saan aru.   saan a·ru

I don't understand.
   Ma ei saa aru.   ma ay saa a·ru

chatting

introductions

Mr	*Härra*	hair·ra
Mrs/Miss	*Proua/Preili*	proh·a/pray·li

How are you?	*Kuidas läheb?*	ku·i·das lair·hep
Fine. And you?	*Hästi. Ja teil?*	hairs·ti ya tayl
What's your name?	*Mis on teie nimi?*	mis on tay·e ni·mi
My name is ...	*Minu nimi on ...*	mi·nu ni·mi on ...
I'm pleased to meet you.	*Meeldiv teid kohata.*	meyl·div tayt ko·hat·ta

Here's my ...	*Siin on minu ...*	seen on mi·nu ...
What's your ...?	*Mis on teie ...?*	mis on tay·e ...
(email) address	*(e-posti) aadress*	(ey·pos·ti) aa·dres
phone number	*telefoninumber*	te·le·fo·ni·num·ber

What's your occupation?
Mis tööd te teete?   mis teud te *teyt*·te

I'm a ...   *Ma olen ...*   ma *o*·len ...
  businessperson   *ärimees* m   *air*·ri·meys
                ärinaine f   *air*·ri·nai·ne
  student   *üliõpilane*   *ew*·li·uh·pi·la·ne

Where are you from?
Kust te pärit olete?   kust te *pair*·rit *o*·let·te
I'm from (England).
Ma olen (Inglismaalt).   ma *o*·len (*ing*·klis·maalt)
Are you married?
Kas te olete abielus?   kas te *o*·let·te *a*·bea·lus
I'm married/single.
Ma olen abielus/   ma *o*·len *a*·bea·lus/
vallaline.   *val*·la·li·ne
How old are you?
Kui vana te olete?   *ku*·i *va*·na te *o*·let·te
I'm ... years old.
Ma olen ...   ma *o*·len ...

making conversation

What's the weather like?
Mis on ilm?   mis on ilm

It's...   *... on.*   ... on
  cold   *Külm*   kewlm
  hot   *Palav*   *pa*·lav

It's raining.   *Sajab vihma.*   *sa*·yab *vikh*·ma
It's snowing.   *Sajab lund.*   *sa*·yab lund

Do you live here?
Kast e elate siin?   kast e *e*·lat·te seen
Where are you going?
Kuhu te lähete?   *ku*·hu te *lair*·het·te
What are you doing?
Mida te teete?   *mi*·da te *teyt*·te

invitations

Would you like	*Kas te sooviksite*	kas te *saw*·vik·sit·te
to go (for a) ...?	*minna ...?*	*min*·na ...
dancing	*tantsima*	*tan*·tsi·ma
drink	*dringile*	*dring*·ki·le
meal	*sööma*	*seu*·ma
out	*kuhugi välja*	*ku*·hu·gi *vair*·lya

Yes, I'd love to.
Jaa, meelsasti.   yaa *meyl*·sas·ti

No, I'm afraid I can't.
Kahjuks ma ei saa.   *kakh*·yuks ma ay saa

I love it here!
Mulle meeldib siin!
mul·le *meyl*·dib seen

What time will we meet?
Mis kell me kohtume?   mis kel me *kokht*·tu·me

Where will we meet?
Kus me kohtume?   kus me *kokht*·tu·me

Let's meet at ...	*Kohtume ...*	*kokht*·tu·me ...
(eight) o'clock	*kell (kaheksa)*	kel (*ka*·hek·sa)
the entrance	*sissepääsu juures*	*sis*·sep·pair·su *yoo*·res

meeting up

Can I ...?	*Kas ma tohin ...?*	kas ma *to*·hin ...
dance with you	*teiega tantsida*	*tay*·e·ga *tan*·tsi·da
sit here	*siia istuda*	*see*·a *is*·tu·da
take you home	*teid koju saata*	tayd *ko*·yu *saat*·ta

I'm here with my girlfriend/boyfriend.
Olen siin oma   *o*·len seen *o*·ma
tüdruksõbraga/   *tewd*·ruk·suh·bra·ga/
poiss-sõbraga.   *poys*·suh·bra·ga

27

It's been great meeting you.
Oli tore teiega kohtuda.   o·li to·re tay·e·ga kokht·tu·da

Keep in touch!
Suhtleme!   sukht·le·me

likes & dislikes

I thought it was ...	*Mu meelst oli see ...*	mu meylst o·li sey ...
It's ...	*On see ...*	on sey ...
awful	*kohutav*	ko·hu·tav
great	*lahe*	la·he
interesting	*huvitav*	hu·vi·tav
Do you like ...?	*Kas teile meeldib ...?*	kas tay·le meyl·dib ...
I like ...	*Mulle meeldib ...*	mul·le meyl·dib ...
I don't like ...	*Ei meeldi ...*	ay meyl·di ...
art	*kunst*	kunst
shopping	*sisseoste teha*	sis·se·os·te te·ha
sport	*sportida*	spor·ti·da

eating & drinking

I'd like ..., please.	*Ma sooviksin ..., palun.*	ma saw·vik·sin ... pa·lun
the nonsmoking section	*mitte suitsetajate osakond*	mit·te su·it·set·ta·yat·te o·sa·kont
the smoking section	*suitsetajate osakond*	su·it·set·ta·yat·te o·sa·kont
a table for (four)	*lauda (neljale)*	low·da (nel·ya·le)

Do you have vegetarian food?
Kas teil on taimetoitu?   kas tayl on tai·met·toyt·tu

What would you recommend?
Mida te soovitate?   mi·da te saw·vit·tat·te

| I'll have a ... | *Ma tahaksin ...* | ma ta·hak·sin ... |
| Cheers! | *Terviseks!* | tair·vi·seks |

I'd like (the) …, please.	Ma sooviksin …, palun.	ma *saw*·vik·sin … *pa*·lun
bill	arvet	ar·vet
drink list	veinikaarti	vay·ni·kaart·ti
menu	menüüd	me·newt
that dish	seda toitu	se·da toyt·tu

Would you like a drink?
Kas te sooviksite üht drinki?
kas te *saw*·vik·sit·te ewkht *dringk*·ki

(cup of) coffee/tea	(tass) kohvi/teed	(tas) kokh·vi/teyd
(mineral) water	(mineraal)vesi	(mi·ne·*raal*·)ve·si
glass of (wine)	klaas (veini)	klaas (*vay*·ni)
bottle of (beer)	pudel (õlut)	pu·del (*uh*·lut)
breakfast	hommikusöök	hom·mi·ku·seuk
lunch	lõuna	luh·u·na
dinner	õhtusöök	uhkh·tu·seuk

Estonian

exploring

Where's the …?	Kus on …?	kus on …
bank	pank	pank
hotel	hotell	ho·tel
post office	postkontor	post·kont·tor

Can you show me (on the map)?
Kas te näitaksite mulle (kaardil)?
kas te *nair*·i·tak·sit·te *mul*·le (*kaar*·dil)

What time does it open/close?
Millal avatakse/suletakse?
mil·lal a·va·tak·se/su·le·tak·se

What's the admission charge?
Mis maksab sissepääs?
mis *mak*·sab sis·sep·pairs

When's the next tour?
Millal on järgmine tiir?
mil·lal on *yairg*·mi·ne teer

29

Where can I find ...?	Kus asuvad ...?	kus *a*·su·vad ...
clubs	klubid	*klu*·bid
gay venues	geiklubid	*gay*·klu·bid
pubs	pubid	*pu*·bid

Can we get there by public transport?

Kas sinna saab ühistranspordiga?	kas *sin*·na saab *ew*·his·trans·por·di·ga

Where can I buy a ticket?

Kust saab osta pileti?	kust saab *os*·ta *pi*·let·ti

One ... ticket (to Pärnu), please.	Üks ... pilet (Pärnusse), palun.	ewks ... *pi*·let (*pair*·nus·se) *pa*·lun
one-way	ühe otsa	*ew*·he *o*·tsa
return	edasi-tagasi	e·da·si·ta·ga·si

My luggage has been ...	Mu pagas on ...	mu *pa*·gas on ...
lost	kadunud	*ka*·du·nud
stolen	varastatud	va·ra·stat·tud

Is this the ... to (Tartu)?	Kas see on (Tartu) ...?	kas sey on (*tar*·tu) ...
boat	laev	laiv
bus	buss	bus
plane	lennuk	*len*·nuk
train	rong	rongk

What time's the ... bus?	Mis kell väljub ... buss?	mis kel *vairl*·yub ... bus
first	esimene	e·si·me·ne
last	viimane	vee·ma·ne
next	järgmine	*yairg*·mi·ne

I'd like a taxi ...	Ma sooviksin taksot ...	ma *saw*·vik·sin *tak*·sot ...
at (9am)	kell (üheksa hommikul)	kel (*ew*·hek·sa *hom*·mik·kul)
tomorrow	homme	*hom*·me

How much is it to ...?

Kui palju maksab ...?	ku·i *pal*·yu *mak*·sab ...

Please take me to (this address).
Palun sõitke (sellel aadressil). pa·lun *suh*·it·ke (*sel*·lel *aa*·dres·sil)

Please stop here.
Palun peatuge siin. pa·lun *pairt*·tu·ge seen

shopping

Where's the (market)?	*Kus on (turg)?*	kus on (turg)
I'm looking for ...	*Ma otsin ...*	ma o·tsin
It's faulty.	*See on vigane.*	sey on *vi*·ga·ne
I'd like ..., please.	*Ma sooviksin ..., palun.*	ma *saw*·vik·sin ... pa·lun
a refund	*oma raha tagasi*	o·ma *ra*·ha *ta*·ga·si
to return this	*selle tagastada*	*sel*·le *ta*·ga·sta·da

How much is it?
Kui palju see maksab? ku·i *pal*·yu sey *mak*·sab

Can you write down the price?
Kirjutage hind, palun. *kir*·yut·ta·ge hint pa·lun

That's too expensive.
See on liiga kallis. sey on *lee*·ga *kal*·lis

There's a mistake in the bill.
Arves on viga. *ar*·ves on *vi*·ga

I need a film for this camera.
Mul oleks vaja filmi mul o·leks *va*·ya *fil*·mi
sellele kaamerale. *sel*·le·le *kaa*·me·ra·le

Do you accept ...?	*Kas te võtate vastu ...?*	kas te *vuh*·tat·te *vas*·tu ...
credit cards	*krediitkaarte*	kre·*deet*·kaar·t·le
travellers cheques	*reisitšekke*	*ray*·si·chek·ke

I'd like ..., please.	*Ma sooviksin ..., palun.*	ma *saw*·vik·sin ... pa·lun
my change	*raha tagasi*	*ra*·ha *ta*·ga·si
a receipt	*kviitungit*	*kvee*·tung·kit

Estonian

working

Where's the (business centre)?
Kus on (ärikeskus)?   kus on (air·ri·kes·kus)

I'm attending a ...   *Osalen ...*   o·sa·len ...
  conference   *konverentsil*   kon·ve·ren·tsil
  course   *kursusel*   kur·su·sel
  meeting   *kohtumisel*   kokh·tu·mi·sel

I'm visiting a trade fair.
Külastan kaubandusmessi.   kew·la·stan kow·ban·dus·mes·si

I have an appointment with ...
Mul on kohtumine ...   mul on kokh·tu·mi·ne ...

I'm with my colleagues.
Olen koos kolleegidega.   o·len kaws kol·ley·gi·de·ga

Here's my business card.
Siin on mu visiitkaart.   seen on mu vi·seet·kaart

That went very well.
Kõik sujus väga hästi.   kuh·ik su·yus vair·ga hairs·ti

emergencies

Help!	*Appi!*	ap·pi
Stop!	*Lõpetage!*	luhp·pe·ta·ge
Go away!	*Minge ära!*	ming·ke air·ra
Thief!	*Varas!*	va·ras
Fire!	*Tulekahju!*	tu·le·kakh·yu
Call ...!	*Kutsuge ...!*	ku·tsu·ge ...
an ambulance	*kiirabi*	kee·ra·bi
a doctor	*arst*	arst
the police	*politsei*	po·li·tsay

Could you help me, please?   *Palun kas te saaksite mind aidata?*   pa·lun kas te saak·sit·te mint ai·dat·ta

I'm lost.   *Ma olen ära eksinud.*   ma o·len air·ra ek·si·nud

Where are the toilets?   *Kus on WC?*   kus on ve·se

Estonian

Faroese

The Faroe Islands are as raw and wild as a
seabird's cry.

Pronunciation

Vowels		Consonants	
Symbol	**English sound**	**Symbol**	**English sound**
a	run	b	bed
ai	aisle	ch	cheat
air	hair	d	dog
ay	say	f	fat
e	bet	g	go
ee	see	h	hat
eu	nurse	j	joke
i	hit	k	kit
iew	view	l	lot
o	pot	m	man
oh	note	n	not
oo	soon	p	pet
ow	how	r	red (trilled)
oy	toy	s	sun
u	put	sh	shot
uh	ago	t	top
ui	as in the Spanish 'muy'	v	very
		w	win
		y	yellow

The Faroese pronunciation is given in purple after each word or phrase. Read these words as though you were reading English and you're sure to be understood. Each syllable is separated by a dot, and italics indicate that you need to put stress on that syllable, for example:

Orsaka. o·*shair*·kuh

essentials

Yes./No.	*Ja./Nei.*	yair/nai
Hello./Goodbye.	*Góðan dag./Farvæl.*	goh·wuhn dair/far·vairl
Please.	*Ger so væl.*	jer so vairl
Thank you (very much).	*Takk (fyri).*	tuhk (fi·ri)
You're welcome.	*Sjálvur/Sjálv takk.* m/f	shol·vur/sholv tuhk
Excuse me./Sorry.	*Orsaka.*	o·shair·kuh
Do you speak English?	*Tosa tygum enskt?*	toh·suh tee·yun enkst
Do you understand?	*Skilja tygum?*	shil·yuh tee·yun
I (don't) understand.	*Eg skilji (ikki).*	e shil·yi (i·chi)

chatting

introductions

Mr	*harra*	huhr·ruh
Mrs	*frú*	friew
Ms	*frøkun*	freu·kun

How are you?
    Hvussu hava tygum tað?   kvus·se he·vuh tee·yun tair

Fine. And you?
    Gott. Og hjá tygum?   got oh chwuh tee·yun

What's your name?
    Hvussu eita tygum?   kvus·se ai·tuh tee·yun

My name is ...
    Eg eiti ...   e ai·ti ...

I'm pleased to meet you.
    Stuttligt at hitta tygum.   stut·lit airt hit·tuh tee·yun

Here's my ...	*Her er ...*	her er ...
(email) address	*mín (teldupost)-adressa*	muin (tel·du·post)·uh·dres·suh
phone number	*mítt telefon-nummar*	moyt te·le·fohn·num·mar

Faroese

35

What's your ...?	Hvat er ...?	kvairt er ...
(email) address	tín (teldupost)-adressa	tuin (tel·du·post)·uh·dres·suh
phone number	títt telefon-nummar	toyt te·le·fohn·num·mar

What's your occupation?
Hvat gera tygum? — kvairt je·ruh tee·yun

I'm a student.
Eg eri studentur. — e e·ri stoo·den·tur

I'm a businessperson.
Eg arbeiði sum handilsmaður/handilskvinna. m/f — e ar·bai·yi sum huhn·dils·mair·vur/huhn·dils·kvin·nuh

Where are you from?
Hvaðani eru tygum? — kvair·uh·ni e·ru tee·yun

I'm from (England).
Eg eri úr (Onglandi). — e e·ri iewr (ong·gluhn·di)

Are you married?
Eru tygum giftur/gift? m/f — e·ru tee·yun jif·tur/jift

I'm married.
Eg eri giftur/gift. m/f — e e·ri jif·tur/jift

I'm single.
Eg eri ógiftur/ógift. m/f — e e·ri oh·jif·tur/oh·jift

How old are you? (to a man)
Hvussu gamal eru tygum? — kvus·se gair·muhl e·ru tee·yun

How old are you? (to a woman)
Hvussu gomul eru tygum? — kvus·se goh·mul e·ru tee·yun

I'm ... years old.
Eg eri ... ára gamal/gomul. m/f — e e·ri ... wuh·ruh gair·muhl/goh·m

making conversation

What's the weather like?
Hvussu er veðrið? — kvus·se er veg·ri

It's ...	Tað er ...	tair er ...
cold	kalt	kuhlt
hot	heitt	hait
raining	regn	regn
snowing	kavi	kair·vi

Do you live here?	Búgva tygum her?	big·vuh tee·yun her
Where are you going?	Hvar ganga tygum til?	kvair geng·ga tee·yun til
What are you doing?	Hvat gera tygum?	kvairt je·ruh tee·yun

invitations

Would you like to go (for a) …?	Skulu vit fara út …?	sku·lu veet fe·ruh iewt …
dancing	og dansa	oh duhn·suh
drink	og hava eitt glas	oh he·vuh ait glairs
meal	og eta	oh air·tuh
out	onkunstaðni	on·kun·stair·ni

Yes, I'd love to.
Ja, tað vil eg gjarna. yair tair vil e juhr·nuh

No, I'm afraid I can't.
Nei, tað kann eg ikki. nai tair kuhn e i·chi

I love it here!
Her er frálíkt!
her er frwuh·loykt

What time will we meet?
Nær klokkan skulu vit møta? nair klok·kuhn sku·lu veet meu·tuh

Where will we meet?
Hvar skulu vit møta? kvair sku·lu veet meu·tuh

Let's meet at …	Vit skulu møta …	veet sku·lu meu·tuh …
(eight) o'clock	klokkan (átta)	klok·kuhn (o·tuh)
the entrance	við inngongdini	vee in·gong·di·ni

meeting up

Can I …?	Fái eg …?	fwuh·i e …
dance with you	dansa við tær	duhn·suh vee tair
sit here	seta meg her	se·tuh may her
take you home	taka teg heim	te·kuh tay haim

37

I'm here with my girlfriend.
Eg eri her við gentu míni.   e *e*·ri her vee *jen*·tu *mui*·ni

I'm here with my boyfriend.
Eg eri her við drongi mínum.   e *e*·ri her vee *dron*·ji *mui*·nun

It's been great meeting you.
Tað var stuttligt at hitta tygum.   tair ver *stut*·lit airt *hit*·tuh *tee*·yun

Keep in touch!
Skriva til mín!   *skree*·vuh til muin

likes & dislikes

I thought it was ...	*Eg helt tað vera ...*	e helt tair *ve*·ruh ...
It's ...	*Tað er ...*	tair er ...
awful	*øgiligt*	*eu*·ji·lit
great	*frálíkt*	*frwuh*·loykt
interesting	*áhugavert*	*wuh*·hoo·uh·vesht
Do you like ...?	*Dámar tær ...?*	*dwuh*·muhr tair ...
I (don't) like ...	*Mær dámar (ikki) ...*	mair *dwuh*·muh (*i*·chi) ...
art	*list*	list
shopping	*at fara til handils*	airt *fe*·ruh til *huhn*·dils
sport	*ítrótt*	*ui*·trot

eating & drinking

A table ..., please.	*Eitt borð ..., takk.*	ait bor ... tuhk
for (four)	*til (fýra)*	til (*fui*·ruh)
in the nonsmoking section	*í roykfríðum øki*	ui *royk*·frui·um *eu*·chi

Do you have vegetarian food?
Hava tygum nakran   *he*·vuh *tee*·yun *ne*·kruhn
mat fyri vegetarar?   mairt *fi*·ri ve·ge·*tuhr*·ruhr

What would you recommend?
Hvat kunnu tygum mæla til?   kvairt *kun*·nu *tee*·yun *me*·luh til

I'll have a ...	*Eg hevði fegin ...*	e *he*·yi *fay*·yin ...
Cheers!	*Skál!*	skwuhl

38

I'd like (the) ..., please.	Kann eg fáa ..., takk?	kuhn e fwuh ... tuhk
bill	rokningina	rok·nin·ji·nuh
drink list	vínkortið	vuin·kosh·ti
menu	matseðilin	mairt·say·i·lin
that dish	handan rættin	huhn·duhn ret·tin

Would you like a drink?
Hevði tær dámt okkurt at drekka?
he·yi tair domt o·kusht airt drek·kuh

(cup of) coffee/tea	(ein kopp av) kaffi/te	(ain kop airv) kuhf·fi/te
(mineral) water	(soda)vatn	(soh·duh·)vatn
bottle of (beer)	eina fløsku av (øli)	ai·nuh fleus·ku airv (eu·li)
glass of (wine)	eitt glas av (víni)	ait glairs airv (vui·ni)

breakfast	morgunmatur	mor·gun·mair·tur
lunch	døgurði	deuv·ri
dinner	nátturði	not·ri

exploring

Where's the ...?	Hvar er ...?	kvair er ...
bank	bankin	buhn·chin
hotel	hotellið	hoh·tel·li
post office	posthúsið	post·hiew·si

Can you show me (on the map)?
Kunnu tygum vísa mær tað (á kortinum)?
kun·nu tee·yun vee·suh mair tair (wuh kosh·ti·nun)

What time does it open/close?
Nær klokkan letur tað upp/aftur? nair klok·kuhn le·tur tair up/uh·tur

What's the admission charge?
Hvussu nógv kostar tað at sleppa inn? kvus·se negv kos·tuhr tair airt slep·puh in

When's the next tour?
Nær klokkan byrjar næsta rundferðin? nair klok·kuhn bir·yuhr nes·tuh rund·fair·in

39

Where can I find ...? *Hvar eru ...?* kvair e·ru ...
clubs *diskotekini* dis·koh·*tair*·chi·ni
pubs *barrirnar* buh·rir·nuhr

Can we get there by public transport?
Er tað møguligt at koma hagar er tair *meuv*·lit airt ko·muh hair·uh
við almennum flutningi? vee *uhl*·me·nun flut·nin·ji

Where can I buy a ticket?
Hvar kann eg keypa ein ferðaseðil? kvair kuhn e *chay*·puh ain fair·ruh·

One ... ticket (to *... til Klaksvíkar),* ... *til kluhks*·vui·kuhr)
Klaksvík), please. *takk.* tuhk
one-way *Einvegis ferðaseðil* ain·vay·yis fair·ruh·say·
return *Ferðaseðil aftur* fair·ruh·say·il uh·tur
og fram oh fruhm

My luggage *Viðførið hjá mær* vee·feu·ri chwuh mair
has been ... *er ...* er ...
lost *burturmist* busht·tur·mist
stolen *stolið* stoh·li

Is this the ... *Er hetta ...* er het·tuh ...
to (Tórshavn)? *(til Tórshavnar)?* (til *torsh*·how·nuhr)
boat *báturin* bwuh·tu·rin
bus *bussurin* bus·su·rin
helicopter *tyrlan* tir·luhn
plane *flogfarið* floh·fair·ri

What time's *Nær fer ...* nair fer ...
the ... bus? *bussurin?* bus·su·rin
first *fyrsti* fis·ti
last *síðsti* sis·ti
next *næsti* nes·ti

I'd like a taxi ... *Eg hevði fegin* e he·yi fay·yin
ein hýruvogn ... ain hui·ru·vogn ...
at (9am) *klokkan (níggju* klok·kuhn (nu·ju
um morgunin) um mor·gu·nin)
tomorrow *í morgin* ui mor·jin

How much is it to ...?
Hvussu nógv kostar tað til ...? kvus·se negv kos·tuhr tair til ...

40

Please take me to (this address).
Koyr meg til (hesa   koyr may til (*he*·suh
adressuna), takk.   uh-*dres*·su·nuh) tuhk

Please stop here.
Steðga her, takk.   stair·guh her tuhk

shopping

Where's the (shopping centre)?
Hvar er (sølumiðstøðin)?   kvair er (*seu*·lu·mi·steu·yin)

I'm looking for …
Eg leiti eftir …   e *lai*·ti et·tir …

It's faulty.
Tað er brákatt.   tair er *brwuh*·kuht

I'd like …, please.	*Eg hevði fegin …*	e *he*·yi *fay*·yin …
a refund	*fingið peningin*	*fin*·ji pe·nin·jin
	aftur	*uh*·tur
to return this	*givið hetta aftur*	*ji*·vi het·tuh *uh*·tur

How much is it?
Hvussu nógv kostar hetta?   *kvus*·se negv *kos*·tuhr het·tuh

Can you write down the price?
Kunnu tygum gera so væl   *kun*·nu tee·yun je·ra so vairl
at skriva prísin?   airt *skree*·vuh *prui*·sin

That's too expensive.
Tað er ov dýrt.   tair er oh dusht

There's a mistake in the bill.
Rokningin er skeiv.   *rok*·nin·jin er skaiv

I need a film for this camera.
Mær tørvar ein film til   mair *teur*·vuhr ain film til
hetta fototólið.   *het*·tuh foh·toh·toh·li

Do you accept …?	*Taka tit …?*	*te*·kuh teet …
credit cards	*gjaldskort*	*juhlds*·kosht
travellers cheques	*ferðakekkar*	*fair*·ruh·chek·kuhr

I'd like …, please.	*Eg hevði fegin …*	e *he*·yi *fay*·yin …
my change	*veksluþeningin*	*veks*·lu·pe·nin·jin
a receipt	*eina kvittan*	*ai*·nuh *kvit*·tuhn

41

working

Where's the (business centre)?
Hvar er (handilsstovan)?   kvair er (*huhn*·dils·stoh·vuhn)

I'm attending a ...   *Eg eri við á ...*   e *e*·ri vee wuh ...
   conference   *eini ráðstevnu*   *ai*·ni *rwuh*·stev·nu
   course   *einum námskeiði*   *ai*·nun nom·skai·yi
   meeting   *einum fundi*   *ai*·nun *fun*·di

I'm visiting a trade fair.
Eg vitji eina handilsmessu.   e *vit*·yi *ai*·nuh *huhn*·dils·mes·su

I have an appointment with ...
Eg havi avtalu hjá ...   e *he*·vi airv·tair·lu chwuh ...

I'm with my colleagues.
Eg eri her við mínum   e *e*·ri her vee *mui*·nun
starvsfelagum.   starvs·fe·lair·vun

Here's my business card.
Her er mítt kort.   her er moyt kosht

That went very well.
Tað gekk sera gott.   tair jek *se*·ruh got

emergencies

Help!	*Hjálp!*	hyolp
Stop!	*Stoppa!*	*stop*·puh
Go away!	*Far burtur!*	fair *bush*·tur
Thief!	*Tjóvur!*	*choh*·vur
Fire!	*Eldur!*	*el*·dur

Call ...!   *Ringið eftir ...!*   *rin*·ji et·tir ...
   an ambulance   *sjúkrabili*   *shiew*·kruh·bee·li
   a doctor   *lækna*   *lek*·nuh
   the police   *løgregluni*   *leug*·reg·lu·ni

Could you help me,   *Kunnu tygum hjálpa*   *kun*·nu *tee*·yun *hyol*·puh
   please?   *mær?*   mair
I'm lost.   *Eg eri vilstur/vilst.* m/f   e *e*·ri *vils*·tur/vilst
Where are the   *Hvar eru vesini?*   kvair *e*·ru *vair*·si·ni
   toilets?

Finnish

Natural beauty, lots of elbow room and the fine art of the sauna make Finland a traveller's dream.

Pronunciation

Vowels		Consonants	
Symbol	**English sound**	**Symbol**	**English sound**
a	act	d	dog
aa	father	g	go
ai	aisle	h	hat
ay	say	k	kit
e	bet	l	lot
ee	see	m	man
eu	nurse	n	not
ew	ee pronounced with rounded lips	p	pet
		r	red (rolled)
i	hit	s	sun
o	pot	t	top
oh	note	v	very
oo	zoo	y	yellow
ow	how		
oy	toy		
u	put		
uh	run		

The Finnish pronunciation is given in purple after each word or phrase. Read these words as though you were reading English and you're sure to be understood. Each syllable is separated by a dot, and italics indicate that you need to put stress on that syllable, for example:

Ole hyvä.   o·le *hew*·va

essentials

Yes./No.	*Kyllä./Ei.*	*kewl*·la/ay
Hello./Goodbye.	*Hei./Näkemiin.*	hay/*na*·ke·meen
Please.	*Ole hyvä.*	o·le *hew*·va
Thank you	*Kiitos*	*kee*·tos
(very much).	*(paljon).*	(*puhl*·yon)
You're welcome.	*Ole hyvä.*	o·le *hew*·va
Excuse me.	*Anteeksi.*	uhn·*tayk*·si
Sorry.	*Anteeksi.*	uhn·*tayk*·si

Do you speak English?
   Puhutko englantia?   *pu*·hut·ko en·gluhn·ti·uh

Do you understand?
   Ymmärrätkö?   *ewm*·mar·rat·keu

I understand.
   Ymmärrän.   *ewm*·mar·ran

I don't understand.
   En ymmärrä.   en *ewm*·mar·ra

chatting

introductions

Mr	*Herra*	*her*·ruh
Mrs	*Rouva*	*roh*·vuh
Ms	*Neiti*	*nay*·ti

How are you?
   Mitä kuuluu?   *mi*·ta *koo*·loo

Fine. And you?
   Hyvää. Entä itsellesi?   *hew*·va en·ta *it*·sel·le·si

What's your name?
   Mikä sinun nimesi on?   *mi*·ka *si*·nun *ni*·me·si on

My name is ...
   Minun nimeni on ...   *mi*·nun *ni*·me·ni on ...

I'm pleased to meet you.
   Hauska tavata.   *hows*·kuh *tuh*·vuh·tuh

45

Here's my ...	Tässä on minun ...	tas·sa on mi·nun ...
(email) address	(sähköposti)-	(sah·keu·pos·ti)·
	osoitteeni	o·soyt·tay·ni
phone number	puhelinnumeroni	pu·he·lin·nu·me·ro·ni
What's your ...?	Mikä on sinun ...?	mi·ka on si·nun ...?
(email) address	(sähköposti)-	(sah·keu·pos·ti)·
	osoitteesi	o·soyt·tay·si
phone number	puhelinnumerosi	pu·he·lin·nu·me·ro·si

| What's your occupation? | Mitä teet työksesi? | mi·ta tayt tew·euk·se·si |

I'm a ...	Olen ...	o·len ...
businessperson	liikealalla	lee·ke·uh·luhl·luh
student	opiskelija	o·pis·ke·li·yuh

Where are you from?
Mistä olet kotoisin?   mis·ta o·let ko·toy·sin

I'm from (England).
Olen (Englannista).   o·len (eng·luhn·nis·tuh)

Are you married?
Oletko naimisissa?   o·let·ko nai·mi·sis·suh

I'm married.
Olen naimisissa.   o·len nai·mi·sis·suh

I'm single.
En ole naimisissa.   en o·le nai·mi·sis·suh

How old are you?
Miten vanha olet?   mi·ten vuhn·huh o·let

I'm ... years old.
Olen ... vuotias.   o·len ... vu·o·ti·uhs

making conversation

What's the weather like?
Millainen ilma siellä on?   mil·lai·nen il·muh si·el·la on

It's ...	Siellä ...	si·el·la ...
cold	on kylmä	on kewl·ma
hot	on kuuma	on koo·ma
raining	sataa	suh·taa
snowing	sataa lunta	suh·taa lun·tuh

Do you live here?	Asutko täällä?	uh·sut·ko tal·la
Where are you going?	Minne olet menossa?	min·ne o·let me·nos·suh
What are you doing?	Mitä sinä teet?	mi·ta si·na tayt

invitations

Would you like	Haluaisitko	huh·lu·ai·sit·ko
to go (for a) …?	lähteä …?	lah·te·a …
dancing	tanssimaan	tuhns·si·maan
drink	oluelle	o·lu·el·le
meal	syömään	sew·eu·man
out	ulos	u·los

Yes, I'd love to.
Mielelläni. mi·e·lel·la·ni

No, I'm afraid I can't.
En valitettavasti voi. en vuh·li·tet·tuh·vuhs·ti voy

I love it here!
Viihdyn täällä erinomaisesti!
veeh·dewn ta·al·la e·ri·no·mai·ses·ti

What time will we meet?
Mihin aikaan tapaamme? mi·hin ai·kaan tuh·paam·me

Where will we meet?
Missä tapaamme? mis·sa tuh·paam·me

Let's meet at …	Tavataan …	tuh·vuh·taan …
(eight) o'clock	kello (kahdeksan)	kel·lo (kuh·dek·suhn)
the entrance	ovella	o·vel·luh

meeting up

Can I …?	Saanko …?	saan·ko …
dance with you	luvan	lu·vuhn
sit here	istua tähän	is·tu·uh ta·han
take you home	saattaa sinut	saat·taa si·nut
	kotiin	ko·teen

47

Finnish

I'm here with my girlfriend/boyfriend.

Olen täällä tyttöystäväni/   o·len *tal*·la *tewt·teu·ews·*ta·va·ni/
poikaystäväni kanssa.   *poy·*kuh·*ews·*ta·va·ni *kuhns·*suh

Keep in touch!

Pidetään yhteyttä.   pi·de·tan *ewh*·te·ewt·ta

It's been great meeting you.

Oli mukava tavata.   o·li mu·kuh·vuh *tuh*·vuh·tuh

likes & dislikes

I thought it was ...	Minusta se oli ...	mi·nus·tuh se o·li ...
It's ...	Se on ...	se on ...
awful	hirveää	*hir*·ve·aa
great	mahtavaa	*muh*·tuh·vaa
interesting	mielenkiintoista	mi·e·len·*keen*·toy·stuh
Do you like ...?	Pidätkö ...?	*pi*·dat·keu ...
I like ...	Pidän ...	pi·dan ...
I don't like ...	En pidä ...	en pi·da ...
art	taiteesta	*tai*·tays·tuh
shopping	shoppailusta	*shop*·pai·lus·tuh
sport	urheilusta	*ur*·hay·lus·tuh

eating & drinking

I'd like ..., please.	Saisinko ...	*sai*·sin·ko ...
the nonsmoking section	savuttomalta puolelta	*suh*·vut·to·muhl·tuh *pu*·o·lel·tuh
the smoking section	tupakoivien puolelta	tu·*puhk*·koy·vi·en *pu*·o·lel·tuh
a table for (four)	pöydän (neljälle)	*peu*·ew·dan (*nel*·yal·le)

Do you have vegetarian food?

Onko teillä kasvisruokia?   on·ko *teyl*·la *kuhs·*vis·ru·o·ki·uh

What would you recommend?

Mitä voit suositella?   *mi*·ta voyt su·o·si·tel·luh

I'll have a ...	Tilaan ...	*ti*·laan ...
Cheers!	Kippis!	*kip*·pis

I'd like (the) …, please.	Saisinko …	*sai*·sin·ko …
bill	*laskun*	*luhs*·kun
drink list	*juomalistan*	yu·o·muh·*lis*·tuhn
menu	*ruokalistan*	ru·o·kuh·*lis*·tuhn
that dish	*tuon ruokalajin*	tu·on ru·o·kuh·*luh*·yin

Would you like a drink?
Haluaisitko jotain juotavaa?
huh·lu·ai·sit·ko *yo*·tain yu·o·tuh·vaa

(cup of) coffee/tea	*(kupin) kahvia/teetä*	(ku·pin) kuh·vi·uh/*tay*·ta
(mineral) water	*(kivennäis)vettä*	(ki·ven·na·is·)*vet*·ta
bottle of (beer)	*pullon (olutta)*	pul·lon (o·lut·tuh)
glass of (wine)	*lasillisen (viiniä)*	luh·sil·li·sen (*vee*·ni·a)

breakfast	*aamiaisen*	*aa*·mi·ai·sen
lunch	*lounaan*	*loh*·naan
dinner	*illallisen*	il·luhl·li·sen

Finnish

exploring

Where's the …?	Missä on …?	*mis*·sa on …
bank	*pankki*	*puhnk*·ki
hotel	*hotelli*	*ho*·tel·li
post office	*postitoimisto*	pos·ti·*toy*·mis·to

Can you show me (on the map)?
Voitko näyttää sen minulle (kartalta)?
voyt·ko na·ewt·ta sen *mi*·nul·le (*kar*·tuhl·tuh)

What time does it open/close?
Mihin aikaan se avataan/ suljetaan?
mi·hin *ai*·kaan se *uh*·vuh·taan/ sul·ye·taan

What's the admission charge?
Mitä sisäänpääsy maksaa?
mi·ta *si*·san·pa·sew muhk·saa

When's the next tour?
Milloin lähtee seuraava kiertoajelu?
mil·loyn *lah*·tay se·u·raa·vuh ki·er·to·uh·ye·lu

49

Where can I find ...? *Mistä löydän ...?* mis·ta *leu*·ew·dan ...
- clubs — *klubit* — *klu*·bit
- gay venues — *gaybaarit* — *gay*·baa·rit
- pubs — *pubit* — *pu*·bit

Can we get there by public transport?
Pääseekö sinne — *paa*·see·keu *sin*·ne
julkisella liikenteellä? — *yul*·ki·sel·luh *lee*·ken·teel·la

Where can I buy a ticket?
Mistä voin ostaa lipun? — *mis*·ta voyn *os*·taa *li*·pun

One ... ticket, please.	*Saisinko yhden ... lipun.*	*sai*·sin·ko *ewh*·den ... *li*·pun
one-way	*yksisuuntaisen*	*ewk*·si·*soon*·tai·sen
return	*meno-paluu*	*me*·no·*pa*·loo

My luggage has been ...	*Matkatavarani ...*	*muht*·kuh·tuh·vuh·ruh·ni ...
lost	*ovat kadonneet*	*o*·vuht *kuh*·don·nayt
stolen	*on varastettu*	on *vuh*·ruhs·tet·tu

Where does this ... go?	*Minne tämä ... menee?*	*min*·ne *ta*·ma ... *me*·nay
boat	*laiva*	*lai*·vuh
bus	*bussi*	*bus*·si
plane	*lentokone*	*len*·to·*ko*·ne
train	*juna*	*yu*·nuh

What time's the ... bus?	*Mihin aikaan lähtee ... bussi?*	*mi*·hin *ai*·kaan *lah*·tay ... *bus*·si
first	*ensimmäinen*	*en*·sim·mai·nen
last	*viimeinen*	*vee*·may·nen
next	*seuraava*	*se*·u·raa·vuh

I'd like a taxi ...	*Haluaisin tilata taksin ...*	*huh*·lu·ai·sin *ti*·luh·tuh *tuhk*·sin ...
at (9am)	*kello (yhdeksäksi aamulla)*	*kel*·lo (*ewh*·dek·sak·si *aa*·mul·luh)
tomorrow	*huomiseksi*	*hu*·o·mi·sek·si

How much is it to ...?
Miten paljon maksaa matka ...? — *mi*·ten *puhl*·yon *muhk*·saa *muht*·kuh ...

Please take me to (this address).
Voitko viedä minut   *voyt·ko vi·e·da mi·nut*
(tähän osoitteeseen).   *(ta·han o·soyt·tay·sayn)*

Please stop here.
Pysähdy tässä.   *pew·sah·dew tas·sa*

shopping

Where's the (market)?
Missä (kauppatori) on?   *mis·sa (kowp·pa·to·ri) on*

I'm looking for ...
Etsin ...   *et·sin ...*

It's faulty.
Se on viallinen.   *se on vi·uhl·li·nen*

I'd like ..., please.	*Haluaisin ...*	*huh·lu·ai·sin ...*
a refund	*vaihtaa tämän*	*vaih·taa ta·man*
to return this	*palauttaa tämän*	*puh·lowt·taa ta·man*

How much is it?
Mitä se maksaa?   *mi·ta se muhk·saa*

Can you write down the price?
Voitko kirjoittaa hinnan   *voyt·ko kir·yoyt·taa hin·nuhn*
lapulle?   *luh·pul·le*

That's too expensive.
Se on liian kallis.   *se on lee·uhn kuhl·lis*

There's a mistake in the bill.
Laskussa on virhe.   *luhs·kus·suh on vir·he*

I need a film for this camera.
Tarvitsen filmin tähän   *tuhr·vit·sen fil·min ta·han*
kameraan.   *kuh·me·raan*

Do you accept ...?	*Voinko maksaa ...?*	*voyn·ko muhk·saa ...*
credit cards	*luottokortilla*	*lu·ot·to·kor·til·luh*
travellers cheques	*matkasekillä*	*muht·kuh·se·kil·la*

I'd like ..., please.	*Saisinko ...*	*sai·sin·ko ...*
my change	*vaihtorahat*	*vaih·to·ruh·huht*
a receipt	*kuitin*	*ku·i·tin*

Finnish

working

Where's the (business centre)?
Missä (ostoskeskus) on?   mis·sa (os·tos·kes·kus) on

I'm attending a ...   *Osallistun ...*   o·suhl·lis·tun ...
   conference   *konferenssiin*   kon·fe·rens·seen
   course   *kurssille*   kurs·sil·le
   meeting   *kokoukseen*   ko·kohk·sayn

I'm visiting a trade fair.
Olen käymässä messuilla.   o·len ka·ew·mas·sa mes·su·il·la

I have an appointment with ...
Olen sopinut tapaamisesta   o·len so·pi·nut tuh·paa·mi·ses·tuh
... kanssa.   ... kuhns·suh

I'm with my colleagues.
Olen täällä kollegoitteni kanssa.   o·len tal·la kol·le·goyt·te·ni kuhns·s▪

Here's my business card.
Tässä on käyntikorttini.   tas·sa on ka·ewn·ti·kort·ti·ni

That went very well.
Sehän meni oikein hyvin.   se·han me·ni oy·kayn hew·vin

emergencies

Help!	*Apua!*	uh·pu·uh
Stop!	*Seis!*	says
Go away!	*Mene pois!*	me·ne poys
Thief!	*Varas!*	vuh·ruhs
Fire!	*Tulipalo!*	tu·li·puh·lo
Call ...!	*Soittakaa paikalle ...!*	soyt·tuh·kaa pai·kuhl·le ...
an ambulance	*ambulanssi*	uhm·bu·luhns·si
a doctor	*lääkäri*	la·ka·ri
the police	*poliisi*	po·lee·si
Could you help me, please?	*Voisitko auttaa minua?*	voy·sit·ko owt·taa mi·nu·uh
I'm lost.	*Olen eksynyt.*	o·len ek·sew·newt
Where are the toilets?	*Missä on WC/vessa?*	mis·sa on vee·seeh/ves·suh

Finnish

Greenlandic

Greenland — the ultimate off-the-planet
trip to the Ultima of Thules.

Pronunciation

Vowels		Consonants	
Symbol	English sound	Symbol	English sound
a	run	f	fat
ā	act	gr	great (guttural)
aa	father	k	kit
aw	saw	l	lot
e	bet	m	man
ee	see	n	not
i	hit	ng	ring
o	pot	p	pet
oo	soon	r	red
u	put	s	sun
uh	ago	t	top
		w	win
		y	yellow

The Greenlandic pronunciation is given in purple after each word or phrase. Read these words as though you were reading English and you're sure to be understood. Word stress is of minor importance in Greenlandic and isn't marked in our pronunciation guides. Each syllable is separated by a dot, and italics indicate pitch (meaning that the syllable is pronounced with a rising tone). For example:

Qujanaq.   gru·yuh·*nak*

essentials

Yes./No.	*Aap./Naamik.*	āp/*nā*·mik
Hello./Goodbye.	*Kutaa./Baaj.*	koo·*tā*/baay
Thank you.	*Qujanaq.*	gru·yuh·*nak*
You're welcome.	*Illillu.*	*is*·slis·slu
Sorry.	*Utoqqatserpunga.*	u·*tor*·gruht·serp·pu·nguh

Do you speak English?
  Tuluttut oqalussinnaavit?   tu·*lut*·tut or·gruh·lus·sin·*nā*·wit

Do you understand?
  Paasiviuk?   *pā*·si·wi·uk

I understand.
  Paasivara.   *pā*·si·wa·ra

I don't understand.
  Paasinngilara.   *pā*·sing·ngi·la·ra

chatting

introductions

How are you?
  Qanoq ippit?   gruh·*nok* ip·pit

Fine. And you?
  Ajunngilanga. Illimmi?   uh·*yung*·ngi·luh·nguh *is*·slim·mi

What's your name?
  Qanoq ateqarpit?   gruh·*nok* uh·te·*grap*·pit

My name is ...
  ... mik ateqarpunga.   ... mik uh·te·*grap*·pu·nguh

I'm pleased to meet you.
  Naapillutit nuanneqaaq.   *nā*·pis·slu·tit nu·*uhn*·ne·graak

Here's my ...	*Tassa ...*	*tuhs*·suh ...
What's your ...?	*... pilara.*	... *pi*·la·ra
email address	*Mailit*	*mey*·lit
phone number	*Telefonit*	te·le·*foo*·nit

What's your occupation?		
Sulerivit?		su·*le*·ri·wit

I'm a student.
| *Ilinniarnertuujuvunga.* | | i·lin·ni·yan·net·*too*·yu·wu·nguh |

I'm a businessperson.
| *Namminersortumi* | | *nuhm*·mi·ners·sot·tu·mi |
| *atorfeqarpunga.* | | uh·*tof*·fe·grap·pu·nguh |

Where are you from?
| *Sumiuuit?* | | su·mi·*yoo*·wit |

I'm from England.
| *Tuluuvunga.* | | tu·*loo*·wu·nguh |

I'm from the USA.
| *Amerikarmiuuvunga.* | | uh·me·ri·kam·mi·*yoo*·wu·nguh |

Are you married?
| *Aappaqarpit?* | | *āp*·pa·grap·pit |

I'm married.
| *Aappaqarpunga.* | | *āp*·pa·grap·pu·nguh |

I'm single.
| *Aappaqanngilanga.* | | *āp*·pa·gruhng·ngi·luh·nguh |

How old are you?
| *Qassinik ukioqarpit?* | | gruhs·si·nik u·ki·yo·*grap*·pit |

I'm ... years old.
| *... nik ukioqarpunga.* | | ... nik u·ki·yo·*grap*·pu·nguh |

making conversation

What's the weather like?
| *Sila qanoq ippa?* | | si·*luh* gruh·*nok* ip·puh |

It's ...

cold	*Nillerpoq.*	*nis*·slerp·pok
hot	*Kiappoq.*	ki·*yuhp*·pok
raining	*Siallerpoq.*	si·*yuhs*·slerp·pok
snowing	*Nittaappoq.*	nit·*tāp*·pok

Do you live here?	*Tamaanimiuuit?*	tuh·*mā*·ni·mi·yoo·wit
Where are you going?	*Sumukarniarpit?*	su·mu·*kan*·ni·yap·pit
What are you doing?	*Sulerivit?*	su·*le*·ri·wit

invitations

Would you like to go dancing?
Qitikkiartorusuppit?
gri·*tik*·ki·yat·to·ru·sup·pit

Would you like to go for a drink?
Ataasinnguarto-
riartorusuppit?
uh·*tā*·sing·ngu·wat·to·
ri·yat·to·ru·sup·pit

Would you like to go for a meal?
Neriartorusuppit?
ne·ri·*yat*·to·ru·sup·pit

Would you like to go out?
Illoqarfiliarusuppit?
is·slo·*graf*·fi·li·ya·ru·sup·pit

I love it here!
Maani nuanneqaaq!
mā·ni nu·wuhn·ner·graak

Yes, I'd love to.
Ilaana, perusoqaanga.
i·*lā*·nuh per·ru·so·*grā*·nguh

No, I'm afraid I can't.
Ajoraluartumik
pisinnaanngilanga.
uh·yo·ruh·lu·*wat*·tu·mik
pi·sin·*nāng*·ngi·luh·nguh

What time will we meet?
Qassinut naapissaagut?
gruhs·si·nut nā·pis·*sā*·gut

Where will we meet?
Sumi naapissaagut?
su·*mi* nā·pis·*sā*·gut

Let's meet at ... ... *naapinniarta.* ... *nā*·pin·ni·yat·tuh
   eight o'clock *Arfineq pingasunut* *af*·fi·nek pi·nguh·su·*nut*
   the entrance *Isaarissap eqqaani* i·*saa*·ris·suhp e·*grā*·ni

meeting up

Can I dance with you?
Avalaassinnaavakkit?
uh·wuh·*lās*·sin·nā·wuhk·kit

Can I sit here?
Tamaanga ingissinnaavunga?
tuh·*mā*·nguh i·ngis·sin·*nā*·wu·nga

Can I take you home?
Angerlaassinnaavakkit?
uh·ngers·*slās*·sin·nā·*wak*·kit

57

I'm here with my girlfriend/boyfriend.
Aappara ilagaara.   āp·pa·ra i·luh·*gaa*·ra

It's been great meeting you.
Naapillutit nuanneqaaq.   nā·pis·slu·tit nu·*wuhn*·ne·graak

Keep in touch!
Takuss'!   tuh·*kus*

likes & dislikes

It's ...

awful	*Nuanninngilaq.*	nu·wuhn·*ning*·ngi·lak
great	*Ajunngeqaaq.*	uh·*yung*·nge·graak
interesting	*Soqutiginarpoq.*	so·gru·ti·gi·*nap*·pok
Do you like ...?	... *mik soqutiginnippit?*	... mik so·gru·ti·*gin*·nip
I like ...	*Soqutiginnippunga ...*	so·gru·ti·gin·*nip*·pu·nga
I don't like ...	*Soqutiginninngilanga ...*	so·gru·ti·gin·*ning*·ngi·luh·nga ...
art	*eqqumiitsulianik*	e·gru·*meet*·su·li·yuh·
shopping	*pisiniartaqattaarnermik*	pi·si·ni·yat·tuh·grat·*taan*·nerm·mik
sport	*timersornermik*	ti·mers·*son*·nerm·mi

eating & drinking

I'd like ..., please.	... *perusuppunga.*	... pe·ru·*sup*·pu·nguh
the nonsmoking section	*Pujortarneq ajortut akornanni*	pu·yot·*tan*·nek uh·*yot*·tut uh·*kon*·nuh
the smoking section	*Pujortartartut akornanni*	pu·yot·*tat*·tat·tut uh·*kon*·nuhn·ni
a table for (four)	*(Sisama)nut*	(si·suh·muh)·*nut*

Do you have vegetarian food?
Neqitaqanngitsortaqarpa?   ne·gri·ta·*gruhng*·ngit·sot·ta·grap·pa

What would you recommend?
Suna innersuutissaviuk?   su·*nuh* in·ners·*soo*·tis·suh·wi·yuk

I'll have a ...	... *pilara.*	... *pi*·la·ra
Cheers!	*Skål!*	skawl

58

I'd like (the) ..., please.	... pilanga.	... pi·luh·*nguh*
bill	*Regningimik*	ra·i·ni·ngi·mik
drink list	*Imigassat allas-*	i·mi·*guhs*·suht *uhs*·slas-
	simaffiannik	si·muhf·fi·yuhn·nik
menu	*Nerisassat allas-*	ner·ri·*suhs*·suht *uhs*·slas-
	simaffiannik	si·muhf·fi·yuhn·nik
that dish	*Nerisassanik*	ner·ri·*suhs*·suh·nik
	imaattunik	i·*māt*·tu·nik

Would you like a drink?
Imerusuppit?
i·me·ru·*sup*·pit

cup of coffee/tea	*kaffimik/tiimik*	*kuhf*·fi·mik/*tee*·mik
mineral water	*dansk vandimik*	duhnsk *wuhn*·i·mik
glass of wine	*viinnimik*	*ween*·ni·mik
bottle of beer	*immiaaqqamik*	im·mi·*yaar*·gruh·mik
breakfast	*ullaakkorsiutinik*	us·*slāk*·kos·si·yu·ti·nik
lunch	*frokostimik*	*fru*·kos·ti·mik
dinner	*unnukkorsiutinik*	*un*·nuk·kos·si·yu·ti·nik

exploring

Where's the ...?	... sumiippa?	... su·*meep*·puh
bank	*Bank*	*bang*·ki
hotel	*Akunnittarfik*	uh·*kun*·nit·taf·fik
post office	*Allakkerisarfik*	*uhs*·sluhk·ker·ri·saf·fik

Can you show me (on the map)?
(Nunap assingani)   (nu·*nap* uhs·si·nguh·ni)
Takutilaarsinnaaviuk?   tuh·ku·ti·*luus*·sin·nā·wi·yuk

What time does it open/close?
Qassinut ammassava/   gruhs·si·nut *uhm*·muhs·suh·wuh/
matussava?   muh·*tus*·suh·wuh

What's the admission charge?
Iserneq qanoq akeqarpa?   i·*sern*·nek gruh·*nok* uh·ke·*grap*·puh

When's the next tour?
Qaqugu aallaqqissava?   gruh·gru·*gu* ās·slar·gris·suh·wuh

59

Where can I find ...?	... sumiippat?	... su·*meep*·puht
clubs	Klubbit	klup·pit
gay venues	Anguteqati- minnoortartut	uh·ngu·te·gruh·ti· min·*nawt*·tat·tut
	naapittarfii	nā·pit·taf·fee
pubs	Imerniartarfiit	i·mern·ni·yat·taf·*feet*

Can we get there by public transport?

Ilaaffigisinnaasatsinnik angallassisoqarpa?	i·*lāf*·fi·gi·sin·nā·suht·sin·nik uh·nguh·*slas*·si·so·grap·pa

Where can I buy a ticket?

Sumi billetisisinnaavunga?	su·*mi* pi·le·ti·si·sin·*nā*·wu·nguh

One ... ticket to Kangeq, please.	Ilaassutissaq ... Kangermut.	i·*lās*·su·tis·sak ... ka·*ngerm*·mut
one-way	siumut	si·yu·*mut*
return	siumut uterlugulu	si·yu·*mut* u·*ters*·slu·gu·

My luggage has been ...	Nassatakka ...	nuhs·suh·tuhk·kuh ...
lost	tammarput	*tuhm*·map·put
stolen	tillitaapput	tis·sli·*tāp*·put

Is this the ... to Kangerlussuaq?	Unaava ... Kangerlussuar- mukartussaq?	u·*nā*·wuh ... kuh·ngers·*slus*·su·warm· mu·kart·tus·sak
boat	angallat	uh·*ngas*·sluht
plane	timmisartoq	*tim*·mi·sat·tok

What time's the ... bus?	Qassinut bussi ... aallassava?	*gruhs*·si·nut *bus*·si ... *ās*·sluhs·suh·wuh
first	siulleq	si·*yus*·slek
last	kingulleq	ki·*ngus*·slek
next	tulleq	*tus*·slek

I'd like a taxi ...	Taxamik bestiller- sinnaavunga ...	*tak*·suh·mik pis·ti·lers· sin·*nā*·wu·nguh ...
at 9am	qulingiluanut	gru·li·ngi·lu·wuh·*nut*
tomorrow	aqagu	uh·gruh·*gu*

How much is it (to Nuussuaq)?

(Nuussuarmut) qanoq akeqarpa?	(*noos*·su·warm·mut) gruh·*nok* uh·ke·*grap*·pa

Please take me to (Katuaq).
(Katua)mukassaanga.   (kuh·tu·wa)·mu·kuhs·*sā*·nga

Please stop here.
Tamaanga.   tuh·*mā*·nguh

shopping

Where's the (market)?
(Neqaarniarfik) sumiippa?   (ne·*graan*·ni·yaf·fik) su·*meep*·puh

I'm looking for ...
... ujarpara.   ... u·*yap*·pa·ra

It's faulty.
Atorsinnaanngilaq.   uh·tos·sin·*nāng*·ngi·lak

I'd like a refund, please.
Akiliummik utertitamik   uh·ki·li·*yum*·mik u·*tert*·ti·tuh·mik
perusukkaluarpunga.   pe·ru·*suk*·kuh·lu·wap·pu·nguh

I'd like to return this, please.
Una utertikkusuk-   u·*nuh* u·*tert*·tik·ku·suk·
kaluarpara.   ka·lu·wap·pa·ra

How much is it?
Qanoq akeqarpa?   gruh·*nok* uh·ke·*grap*·puh

Can you write down the price?
Akia allassinnaaviuk?   uh·ki·*yuh* uhs·slas·sin·*nā*·wi·yuk

That's too expensive.
Akisuallaarpoq.   uh·ki·su·wuhs·*slaap*·pok

There's a mistake in the bill.
Regning ajorpoq.   ra·i·ni·ngi uh·*yop*·pok

I need a film for this camera.
Assiliiviup tamatuma   uhs·si·*lee*·wi·yup tuh·*muh*·tu·muh
filmissaa pisiarissavara.   fil·mis·*sā* pi·si·ya·*ris*·suh·wa·ra

Do you accept ...?	*... atorpat?*	... uh·*top*·puht
credit cards	*Akiliissutit*	uh·ki·*lees*·su·tit
travellers cheques	*Rejsecheckit*	ra·i·se·sye·kit

I'd like ..., please.		
my change	*Utertut pilakka.*	u·*tert*·tut pi·*luhk*·kuh
a receipt	*Kvittering pilara.*	kwit·*te*·ri·ngi *pi*·la·ra

working

I'm attending a ...	... peqataaffigaara.	pe·gruh·*táf*·fi·gaa·ra
conference	Ataatsimeersuarneq	uh·*tát*·si·meers·su·wa
course	Pikkorissarneq	pik·ko·*ris*·san·nek
meeting	Ataatsimiinneq	uh·*tát*·si·meen·nek

Where's the (business centre)?
(Ini allaffigisassaq) sumiippa? (i·ni uhs·*sluhf*·fi·gi·suhs·sak) su·*meep*

I'm visiting a trade fair.
Niuffatitsinertalimmik   ni·yuf·fuh·tit·si·nert·tuh·*lim*·mik
saqqummersitsineq   sar·*grum*·mers·sit·si·nek
tikeraarpara.   ti·ke·*raap*·pa·ra

I have an appointment with ...
... isumaqatigiissu   ... i·su·ma·gruh·ti·*gees*·su·
teqarfigaara.   te·*graf*·fi·gaa·ra

I'm with my colleagues.
Suleqatikka ilagaakka.   su·le·gra·*tik*·kuh i·luh·*gák*·kuh

Here's my business card.
Visitkortiga takanna.   wi·*sit*·kor·ti·guh tuh·*kuhn*·nuh

That went very well.
Ingerlalluaqaaq.   i·ngers·slas·slu·wa·*graak*

emergencies

Help!	*Ikiortissannik!*	i·ki·*yot*·tis·suhn·nik
Stop!	*Unigit!*	u·ni·*git*
Go away!	*Peerit!*	*peer*·rit
Thief!	*Tillinniartoqarpoq!*	tis·*slin*·ni·yar·to·grap·pok
Fire!	*Ikuallattoorpoq!*	i·ku·wuhs·sluht·*tawp*·pok

Call ...!	... *sianerfiguuk!*	... si·yuh·nerf·fi·*gook*
an ambulance	Ambulance	am·pu·*lang*·si
a doctor	Nakorsaq	nuh·*kos*·sak

Call the police!	*Politiit sianerfigikkit!*	pu·li·*teet* si·yuh·*nerf*·fi·gik·k
Could you help me, please?	*Ikiulaarsinnaavinga?*	i·ki·yu·*laas*·sin·nä·wi·nguh
I'm lost.	*Tammarpunga.*	tuhm·map·pu·nguh
Where are the toilets?	*Sumi anartarfeqarpa?*	su·*mi* uh·nat·taf·fe·grap·puh

Icelandic

Bathe in the glow of the Midnight Sun and the Northern Lights in Iceland, maybe with some hot mud in between.

Pronunciation

Vowels		Consonants	
Symbol	**English sound**	**Symbol**	**English sound**
a	act	b	bed
ai	aisle	d	dog
ay	say	dh	that
e	bet	f	fat
ee	see	g	go
eu	nurse	h	hat
i	hit	k	kit
o	pot	kh	as the 'ch' in the Scottish *loch*
oh	note		
oo	soon	l	lot
ow	how	m	man
öy	her year (without the 'r')	n	not
		p	pet
u	put	r	red (trilled)
		s	sun
		t	top
		th	thin
		v	very
		y	yellow

The Icelandic pronunciation is given in purple after each word or phrase. Read these words as though you were reading English and you're sure to be understood. Each syllable is separated by a dot, and italics indicate that you need to put stress on that syllable, for example:

Afsakið.   *af*·sa·kidh

Icelandic

essentials

Yes./No.	*Já./Nei.*	yow/nay
Hello./Goodbye.	*Halló./Bless.*	ha·loh/bles
Please.	*Takk.*	tak
Thank you	*Takk (kærlega)*	tak (*kair*·le·ga)
(very much).	*fyrir.*	*fi*·rir
You're welcome.	*Það var ekkert.*	thadh var *e*·kert
Excuse me.	*Afsakið.*	*af*·sa·kidh
Sorry.	*Fyrirgefðu.*	*fi*·rir·gev·dhu

Do you speak English?
   Talar þú ensku?   *ta*·lar thoo *ens*·ku
Do you understand?
   Skilur þú?   *ski*·lur thoo
I (don't) understand.
   Ég skil (ekki).   yekh skil (*e*·ki)

chatting

introductions

Mr	*Herra*	*her*·ra
Mrs/Ms	*Frú*	froo

How are you?
   Hvað segir þú gott?   kvadh *se*·yir thoo got
Fine. And you?
   Allt fínt. En þú?   alt feent en thoo
What's your name?
   Hvað heitir þú?   kvadh *hay*·tir thoo
My name is ...
   Ég heiti ...   yekh *hay*·ti ...
I'm pleased to meet you.
   Gleður mig að   *gle*·dhur mikh adh
   kynnast þér.   *ki*·nast thyer

Here's my ...	Hér er ... mitt.	hyer er ... mit
What's your ...?	Hvert er ... þitt?	kvert er ... thit
address	heimilisfangið	hay·mi·lis·fan·gidh
email address	netfangið	net·fan·gidh
phone number	símanúmerið	see·ma·noo·me·ridh

| What's your occupation? | Hvað vinnur þú við? | kvadh vin·nur thoo vidh |

I'm a ...	Ég er ...	yekh er ...
businessperson	í viðskiptum	ee vidh·skif·tum
student	nemandi	ne·man·di

Where are you from?
Hvaðan kemur þú? — kva·dhan ke·mur thoo

I'm from (England).
Ég er frá (Englandi). — yekh er frow (eng·lan·di)

Are you married?
Ertu giftur/gift? m/f — er·tu gif·tur/gift

I'm married.
Ég er giftur/gift. m/f — yekh er gif·tur/gift

I'm single.
Ég er einhleypur/einhleyp. m/f — yekh er ayn·hlay·pur/ayn·hlayp

How old are you?
Hvað ertu gamall/gömul? m/f — kvadh er·tu ga·matl/geu·mul

I'm ... years old.
Ég er ... ára gamall/gömul. m/f — yekh er ... ow·ra ga·matl/geu·mul

making conversation

What's the weather like?
Hvernig er veðrið? — kver·nikh er vedh·ridh

It's ...	Það er ...	thadh er ...
cold	kalt	kalt
hot	hlýtt	hleet
raining	rigning	rig·ning
snowing	snjókoma	snyoh·ko·ma

Do you live here?	*Býr þú hér?*	beer thoo hyer
Where are you going?	*Hvert ert þú að fara?*	kvert ert thoo adh *fa*·ra
What are you doing?	*Hvað ert þú að gera*	kvadh ert thoo adh *ge*·ra

invitations

Would you like to go (for a) …?	*Vilt þú fara …?*	vilt thoo *fa*·ra …
dancing	*að dansa*	adh *dan*·sa
drink	*að drekka*	adh *dre*·ka
meal	*að borða*	adh *bor*·dha
out	*út*	oot

Yes, I'd love to.
Já, mér list vel á það. yow myer list vel ow thadh

No, I'm afraid I can't.
Nei, því miður get ég það ekki. nay thvee *mi*·dhur get yekh thadh *e*·ki

I love it here!
Ég elska það hérna!
yekh *els*·ka thadh *hyer*·na

What time will we meet?
Klukkan hvað viltu hittast? *klu*·kan kvadh *vil*·tu *hi*·tast

Where will we meet?
Hvar eigum við að hittast? kvar *ay*·yum vidh adh *hi*·tast

Let's meet at …	*Hittumst …*	*hi*·tumst …
(eight) o'clock	*klukkan (átta)*	*klu*·kan (*ow*·ta)
the entrance	*við innganginn*	vidh *in*·gown·gin

meeting up

Can I …?	*Má ég …?*	mow yekh …
dance with you	*dansa við þig*	*dan*·sa vidh thikh
sit here	*sitja hér*	*sit*·ya hyer
take you home	*fylgja þér heim*	*filg*·ya thyer haym

67

I'm here with my girlfriend.
Ég er hér með kærustunni minni. yekh er hyer medh *kai*-rus-*tu*-ni m...

I'm here with my boyfriend.
Ég er hér með kærastanum mínum. yekh er hyer medh *kai*-ras-*ta*-num mee-num

It's been great meeting you.
Það var gaman að hitta þig. thadh var *ga*-man adh *hi*-ta thikh

Keep in touch!
Verum í sambandi! ve-rum ee *sam*-ban-di

likes & dislikes

I thought it was ...	*Mér fannst það ...*	myer fanst thadh ...
It's ...	*Það er ...*	thadh er ...
awful	*vont*	vont
great	*frábært*	*frow*-bairt
interesting	*áhugavert*	*ow*-hu-ga-vert

Do you like ...?	*Finnst þér gaman að ...?*	finst thyer *ga*-man adh ...
I (don't) like ...	*Mér finnst (ekki) gaman að ...*	myer finst (*e*-ki) *ga*-man adh ...
art	*myndlist*	*mind*-list
shopping	*versla*	*vers*-la
sport	*íþróttum*	ee-*throh*-tum

eating & drinking

I'd like ..., please.	*Get ég fengið ..., takk.*	get yekh *fen*-gidh ... tak
the nonsmoking section	*reyklaust borð*	*rayk*-löyst bordh
the smoking section	*borð þar sem má reykja*	bordh thar sem mow *rayk*-ya
a table for (four)	*borð fyrir (fjóra)*	bordh *fi*-rir (*fyoh*-ra)

Do you have vegetarian food?
Hafið þið grænmetisrétti? ha-vidh thidh *grain*-me-tis-rye-ti

What would you recommend?
Hverju mælir þú með? kver-yu *mai*-lir thoo medh

| I'll have a ... | Ég ætla að fá ... | yekh *ait*·la adh fow ... |
| Cheers! | Skál! | skowl |

I'd like (the) ...,	Get ég fengið	get yekh *fen*·gidh
please.	... takk.	... tak
bill	reikninginn	*rayk*·nin·gin
drink list	vínseðillinn	*veen*·se·dhit·lin
menu	matseðillinn	*mat*·se·dhit·lin
that dish	þennan rétt	*the*·nan ryet

Would you like a drink?
Má bjóða þér eitthvað að drekka?
mow *byoh*·dha thyer *ayt*·kvadh adh *dre*·ka

(cup of) coffee/tea	kaffi/te (bolla)	*ka*·fi/te (*bot*·la)
(mineral) water	vatn	vat
bottle of (beer)	(bjór)flösku	(*byohr*)·*fleus*·ku
glass of (wine)	(vín)glas	(*veen*)·glas
breakfast	morgunmat	*mor*·gun·mat
lunch	hádegismat	*how*·de·yis·mat
dinner	kvöldmat	*kveuld*·mat

exploring

Where's the ...?	Hvar er ...?	kvar er ...
bank	bankinn	*bown*·kin
hotel	hótelið	*hoh*·te·lidh
post office	pósthúsið	*pohst*·hoo·sidh

Can you show me (on the map)?
Geturðu synt mér (á kortinu)?   ge·tur·dhu seent myer (ow *kor*·ti·nu)

What time does it open/close?
Hvenær opnar/lokar?   kve·nair *op*·nar/*lo*·kar

What's the admission charge?
Hvað kostar inn?   kvadh *kos*·tar in

When's the next tour?
Hvenær er næsta ferð?   kve·nair er *nais*·ta ferdh

Where can I find ...? | *Hvar eru ... ?* | kvar e·ru ...
clubs	*skemmtistaðir*	skem·tis·ta·dhir
gay venues	*staðir fyrir*	sta·dhir fi·rir
	samkynhneigða	sam·kin·hnaykh·dha
pubs	*krár*	krowr

Can we get there by public transport?
Er hægt að taka rútu þangað? — er haikht adh ta·ka roo·tu thown·gad

Where can I buy a ticket?
Hvar kaupi ég miða? — kvar köy·pi yekh mi·dha

My luggage has been stolen.
Farangrinum mínum hefur verið stolið. — fa·rang·ri·num mee·num he·vur ve·ridh sto·lidh

I have lost my luggage.
Ég hef týnt farangrinum mínum. — yekh hef teent fa·rang·ri·num mee·num

One ... ticket (to Reykjavik), please. | *Einn miða ... (til Reykjavíkur), takk.* | aitn ... mi·dha (til rayk·ya·vee·kur) tak
| one-way | *aðra leiðina* | adh·ra lay·dhi·na |
| return | *fram og til baka* | fram okh til ba·ka |

Is this the ... to (Akureyri)? | *Er þetta ... til (Akureyrar)?* | er the·ta ... til (a·ku·ray·rar)
boat	*ferjan*	fer·yan
bus	*rútan*	roo·tan
plane	*flugvélin*	flukh·vye·lin

What time's the ... bus? | *Hvenær fer ... strætisvagninn?* | kve·nair fer ... strai·tis·vag·nin
first	*fyrsti*	firs·ti
last	*síðasti*	see·dhas·ti
next	*næsti*	nais·ti

I'd like a taxi ... | *Get ég fengið leigubíl ...* | get yekh fen·gidh lay·gu·beel ...
| at (9am) | *klukkan (níu fyrir hádegi)* | klu·kan (nee·u fi·rir how·de·yi) |
| tomorrow | *á morgun* | ow mor·gun |

How much is it to ...?
   Hvað kostar til ... ?   kvadh *kos*·tar til ...

Please take me to (this address).
   Viltu aka mér til (þessa staðar)?   *vil*·tu *a*·ka myer til (*the*·sa *sta*·dhar)

Please stop here.
   Stoppaðu hér, takk.   *sto*·pa·dhu hyer tak

shopping

Where's the (market)?
   Hvar er (markaðurinn)?   kvar er (*mar*·ka·dhu·rin)

I'm looking for ...
   Ég leita að ...   yekh *lay*·ta adh ...

It's faulty.
   Það er gallað.   thadh er *gat*·ladh

I'd like ..., please.	*Ég vil ..., takk.*	yekh vil ... tak
a refund	*fá endurgreitt*	fow en·dur·grayt
to return this	*skila þessu*	*ski*·la *the*·su

How much is it?
   Hvað kostar þetta?   kvadh *kos*·tar *the*·ta

Can you write down the price?
   Geturðu skrifað verðið?   *ge*·tur·dhu *skri*·vadh *ver*·dhidh

That's too expensive.
   Þetta er of dýrt.   *the*·ta er of deert

There's a mistake in the bill.
   Það er villa í reikningnum.   thadh er *vit*·la ee *rayk*·ning·num

I need a film for this camera.
   Ég þarf filmu í þessa   yekh tharf *fil*·mu ee *the*·sa
   myndavél.   *min*·da·vyel

Do you accept ...?	*Tekur þú ...?*	*te*·kur thoo ...
credit cards	*kreditkort*	*kre*·dit·kort
travellers cheques	*ferðamannatékka*	*fer*·dha·ma·na·tye·ka

I'd like ..., please.	*Ég vil fá ..., takk.*	yekh vil fow ... tak
my change	*afganginn*	*av*·gown·gin
a receipt	*kvittun*	*kvi*·tun

Icelandic

71

working

Where's the (business centre)?
Hvar er (ráðstefnumiðstöðin)? kvar er (rowdh·step·nu·midh·steu·dhir

I'm attending a ... *Ég sæki ...* yekh *sai*·ki ...
    conference *ráðstefnu* *rowdh·step·nu*
    course *námskeið* *nowm·skaydh*
    meeting *fund* fund

I'm visiting a trade fair.
Ég er á kaupstefnu. yekh er ow *köyp·*step·nu

I have an appointment with ...
Ég á bókaðan fund með ... yekh ow *boh·*ka·dhan fund medh ...

I'm with my colleagues.
Ég er með félögum mínum. yekh er medh *fye·*leu·khum *mee·*num

Here's my business card.
Hér er nafnspaldið mitt. hyer er *nap·*spal·didh mit

That went very well.
Þetta gekk mjög vel. *the·*ta gek myeukh vel

emergencies

Help!	*Hjálp!*	hyowlp
Stop!	*Hættu!*	*hai·*tu
Go away!	*Farðu!*	*far·*dhu
Thief!	*Þjófur!*	*thyoh·*vur
Fire!	*Eldur!*	*el·*dur

Call ...! *Hringdu á ...!* *hring·*du ow ...
    an ambulance *sjúkrabíl* *syoo·*kra·beel
    a doctor *lækni* *laik·*ni
    the police *lögregluna* *leu·*rekh·lu·na

Could you help me, please?
Geturðu hjálpað mér, takk? ge·*tur·*dhu *hyowl·*padh myer tak

I'm lost.
Ég er villtur/villt. m/f yekh er *vil·*tur/vilt

Where are the toilets?
Hvar er snyrtingin? kvar er *snir·*tin·gin

72

Latvian

A vibrant coastal capital, photogenic
castles, music festivals and scenic river
valleys – what more could you want from
Latvia?

Pronunciation

Vowels		Consonants	
Symbol	English sound	Symbol	English sound
a	run	b	bed
aa	father	ch	cheat
ai	aisle	d	dog
air	fair	dy	and you
aw	law	dz	sounds
ay	say	f	fat
e	bet	g	go
ea	ear	h	hat
ee	see	j	joke
i	hit	k	kit
o	pot	l	lot
oo	zoo	ly/l'	million
ow	how	m	man
u	put	n	not
wa	water	ny/n'	canyon

The Latvian pronunciation is given in purple after each word or phrase. Read these words as though you were reading English and you're sure to be understood. Each syllable is separated by a dot, and italics indicate that you need to put stress on that syllable, for example:

Lūdzu. *loo*·dzu

Note that in some words the symbols l' and n' are used instead of ly and ny respectively, to avoid mispronunciation.

p	pet
r	red (trilled)
s	sun
sh	shot
t	top
ts	hats
ty	meet you
v	very
y	yellow
z	zero
zh	pleasure

essentials

Yes./No.	*Jā./Nē.*	yaa/nair
Hello./Goodbye.	*Sveiks./Atā.*	svayks/*a*·taa
Please.	*Lūdzu.*	loo·dzu
Thank you (very much).	*(Liels) Paldies.*	(leals) *pal*·deas
You're welcome.	*Lūdzu.*	loo·dzu
Excuse me.	*Atvainojiet.*	at·vai·nwa·yeat
Sorry.	*Piedodiet.*	pea·dwa·deat

Do you speak English?
Vai Jūs runājat angliski?   vai yoos ru·*naa*·yat *ang*·li·ski

Do you understand?
Vai Jūs saprotat?   vai yoos sa·*prwa*·tat

I (don't) understand.
Es (ne)saprotu.   es (*ne*·)sa·prwa·tu

chatting

introductions

Mr	*Kungs*	kungs
Mrs/Miss	*Kundze/Jaunkundze*	*kun*·dze/*yown*·kun·dze
How are you?	*Kā Jums klājas?*	kaa yums *klaa*·yas
Fine. And you?	*Labi. Un Jums?*	*la*·bi un yums
What's your name?	*Kā Jūs sauc?*	kaa yoos sowts
My name is …	*Mani sauc …*	*ma*·ni sowts …
I'm pleased to meet you.	*Prieks iepazīties.*	preaks *ea*·pa·zee·teas
Here's my …	*Šeit ir mans/ mana …* m/f	shayt ir mans/ *ma*·na …
What's your …?	*Kas ir Jūsu …?*	kas ir *yoo*·su …
(email) address	*(e-pasta) adrese* f	(*air*·pa·sta) *a*·dre·se
phone number	*telefona numurs* m	te·le·*faw*·na *nu*·murs

What's your occupation?
Ar ko Jūs nodarbojaties? — ar kwa yoos *nwa*·dar·bwa·ya·teas

I'm a ...	*Es esmu ...*	es *es*·mu ...
businessperson	*komersants* m	*ko*·mer·sants
	komersante f	*ko*·mer·san·te
student	*students* m	*stu*·dents
	studente f	*stu*·den·te

Where are you from?
No kurienes Jūs esat? — nwa *ku*·rea·nes yoos e·*sat*

I'm from (England).
Es esmu no (Anglijas). — es *es*·mu nwa (*ang*·li·yas)

Are you married?
Vai Jūs esat precējies/ — vai yoos e·*sat* pre·tsair·*yeas*/
precējusies? m/f — pre·tsair·yu·seas

I'm married.
Es esmu precējies/ — es *es*·mu pre·tsair·*yeas*/
precējusies. m/f — pre·tsair·yu·seas

I'm single.
Es esmu neprecēts/ — es *es*·mu ne·pre·*tsairts*/
neprecēta. m/f — ne·pre·tsair·ta

How old are you?
Cik Jums ir gadu? — tsik yums ir *ga*·du

I'm ... years old.
Man ir ... gadu. — man ir ... *ga*·du

making conversation

What's the weather like?
Kāds ir laiks? — kaats ir laiks

It's ...	*Ir ...*	ir ...
cold	*auksts*	owksts
hot	*karsts*	karsts
raining	*lietains*	*lea*·tains
snowing	*sniegains*	*snea*·gains

Do you live here?
Vai Jūs šeit dzīvojat? — vai yoos shayt *dzee*·vwa·yat

Where are you going?
Kur Jūs ejat? kur yoos *e*·yat

What are you doing?
Ko Jūs darat? kwa yoos *da*·rat

invitations

Would you like	*Vai Jūs vēlaties*	vai yoos *vair*·la·teas
to go (for a) …?	*iet …?*	eat …
dancing	*dejot*	*de*·ywat
drink	*iedzert*	*ea*·dzert
meal	*paēst*	*pa*·airst
out	*kautkur*	*kowt*·kur

Yes, I'd love to.
Jā, es ļoti gribētu. yaa es *l'wa*·ti *gri*·bair·tu

No, I'm afraid I can't.
Nē, es diemžēl nevaru. nair es *deam*·zhairl *ne*·va·ru

I love it here!
Man te patīk!
man te *pa*·teek

What time will we meet?
Cikos mēs tiksimies? tsi·kwas mairs *tik*·si·meas

Where will we meet?
Kur mēs tiksimies? kur mairs *tik*·si·meas

Let's meet at …	*Tiksimies …*	tik·si·meas …
(eight) o'clock	*(pūlkstens) astoņos*	(*pook*·stens) *as*·twa·n'was
the entrance	*pie ieejas*	pea *ea*·e·yas

meeting up

Can I …?	*Vai es varu …?*	vai es *va*·ru …
dance with you	*dejot ar Jums*	*dey*·wat ar yums
sit here	*šeit sēdēt*	shayt *sair*·dairt
take you home	*Jūs aizvest mājās*	yoos *aiz*·vest *maa*·yaas

77

Latvian

I'm here with my girlfriend/boyfriend.
Esmu šeit ar draudzeni/draugu. es·mu shayt ar *drow·*dze·ni/*drow·g*

It's been great meeting you.
Ir bijis prieks iepazīties. ir *bi·*yis preaks *ea·*pa·zee·teas

Keep in touch!
Sazināmies! sa·zi·na·meas

likes & dislikes

I thought	*Es domāju ka*	es *dwa·*maa·yu ka
it was ...	*bija ...*	*bi·*ya ...
It's ...	*Ir ...*	ir ...
awful	*draumīgs*	*drow·*smeeks
great	*izcils*	*iz·*tsils
interesting	*interesanti*	*in·*te·re·san·ti
Do you like ...?	*Vai Jums patīk ...?*	vai yums *pa·*teek ...
I like ...	*Man patīk ...*	man *pa·*teek ...
I don't like ...	*Man nepatīk ...*	man *ne·*pa·teek ...
art	*māksla*	*maak·*sla
shopping	*iepirkties*	*ea·*pirk·teas
sport	*sports*	sports

eating & drinking

I'd like ..., please.	*Es vēlos ... lūdzu.*	es *vair·*lwas ... *loo·*dzu
the nonsmoking	*nesmēķētāju*	*ne·*smair·tyair·taa·yu
section	*pusē*	*pu·*sair
the smoking	*smēķētāju*	*smair·*tyair·taa·yu
section	*pusē*	*pu·*sair
a table for (four)	*galdu (četriem)*	*gal·*du (*chet·*ream)

Do you have vegetarian food?
Vai Jums ir veģetārie ēdieni? vai yums ir *ve·*dye·taa·rea *air·*dea·ni

What would you recommend?
Ko Jūs iesakat? kwa yoos *ea·*sa·kat

I'll have a ... *Man lūdzu vienu ...* man *loo·*dzu *vea·*nu ...
Cheers! *Priekā!* *prea·*kaa

I'd like (the) ..., please.	Es vēlos ..., lūdzu.	es *vair*·lwas ... *loo*·dzu
bill	rēķinu	*rair*·tyi·nu
drink list	dzērienkarti	dzair·rean·kar·ti
menu	ēdienkarti	air·dean·kar·ti
that dish	šo ēdienu	shwa *air*·dea·nu

Would you like a drink?
Vai Jūs vēlaties dzert?
vai yoos *vair*·la·teas dzert

cup of coffee/tea	tasi kafijas/tējas	ta·si ka·fi·yas/*tair*·yas
(mineral) water	(minerālo) ūdeni	(*mi*·ne·raa·lwa) oo·de·ni
glass of (wine)	glāzi (vīnu)	glaa·zi (*vee*·nu)
bottle of (beer)	pudeli (alu)	pu·de·li (*a*·lu)
breakfast	brokastis	brwa·ka·stis
lunch	pusdienas	pus·dea·nas
dinner	vakariņas	va·ka·ri·nyas

exploring

Where's the ...?	Kur ir ...?	kur ir ...
bank	banka	*ban*·ka
hotel	viesnīca	veas·nee·tsa
post office	pasts	pasts

Can you show me (on the map)?
Vai Jūs varat man parādīt (uz kartes)?
vai yoos va·rat man pa·raa·deet (uz *kar*·tes)

What time does it open/close?
Cikos ir vaļā/slēdz?
tsi·kwas ir va·*lyaa*/slairdz

What's the admission charge?
Cik maksā ieeja?
tsik *mak*·saa ea·e·ya

When's the next tour?
Cikos būs nākamā ekskursija?
tsi·kwas boos *naa*·ka·maa eks·kur·si·ya

Latvian

79

Where can I find ...?	Kur es varu meklēt ...?	kur es va·ru me·klairt ...
clubs	klubus	klu·bus
gay venues	geija klubus	ge·ya klu·bus
pubs	krogus	krwa·gus

Can we get there by public transport?

Vai mēs tur tiekam ar sabiedrisko transportu?	vai mairs tur tea·kam ar sa·bea·dris·kwa tran·spor·tu

Where can I buy a ticket?

Kur es varu nopirkt biļeti?	kur es va·ru nwa·pirkt bi·lye·ti

One ... ticket (to Jūrmala), please.	Vienu ... biļeti (uz Jūrmalu), lūdzu.	vea·nu ... bi·lye·ti (uz yoor·ma·lu) loo·dzu
one-way	vienvirziena	vean·vir·zea·na
return	turp-atpakaļ	turp·at·pa·kal'

My luggage has been ...	Mana bagāža ir ...	ma·na ba·gaa·zha ir ...
lost	pazudusi	pa·zu·du·si
stolen	nozagta	nwa·zag·ta

Is this the ... to (Liepāja)?	Vai šis/šī ir ... uz (Liepāju)? m/f	vai shis/shee ir ... uz (lea·paa·yu)
boat	laiva f	lai·va
bus	autobus m	ow·to·bus
plane	lidmašīna f	lid·ma·shee·na
train	vilciens m	vil·tseans

What time's the ... bus?	Cikos ir ... autobus?	tsi·kwas ir ... ow·to·bus
first	pirmais	pir·mais
last	pēdejais	pair·de·yais
next	nākamais	naa·ka·mais

I'd like a taxi ...	Es vēlos taksi ...	es vair·lwas tak·si ...
at (9am)	(deviņos no rīta)	(de·vi·n'was no ree·ta)
tomorrow	rītā	ree·taa

How much is it to ...?

Cik maksā līdz ...?	tsik mak·saa leedz ...

Please take me to (this address).
    Lūdzu aizvediet mani uz   loo·dzu aiz·ve·deat ma·ni uz
    (šo adresi).   (shwa a·dre·si)

Please stop here.
    Lūdzu pieturiet šeit.   loo·dzu pea·tu·reat shayt

shopping

Where's the (market)?	*Kur ir (tirgus)?*	kur ir (tir·gus)
I'm looking for …	*Es meklēju …*	es mek·lair·yu …
It's faulty.	*Ir bojāts.*	ir bwa·yaats
I'd like …, please.	*Es vēlos …, lūdzu.*	es vair·lwas … loo·dzu
a refund	*atmaksu*	at·mak·su
to return this	*šo atgriezt*	shwa at·greast

How much is it?
    Cik maksā?   tsik mak·saa

Can you write down the price?
    Vai Jūs uzrakstīsiet cenu?   vai yoos uz·rak·stee·seat tse·nu

That's too expensive.
    Tas ir par dārgu.   tas ir par daar·gu

There's a mistake in the bill.
    Rēķinā ir kļūda.   rair·tyi·naa ir klyoo·da

I need a film for this camera.
    Man vajag filmu šai   man va·yag fil·mu shai
    kamerai.   ka·me·rai

Do you accept …?	*Vai Jūs ņemat …?*	vai yoos nye·mat …
credit cards	*kredītkartes*	kre·deet·kar·tes
travellers cheques	*ceļojuma čekus*	tse·l'wa·yu·ma che·kus
I'd like …, please.	*Es vēlos …, lūdzu.*	es vair·lwas … loo·dzu
my change	*manu sīknaudu*	ma·nu seek·now·du
a receipt	*kvīti*	kvee·ti

working

Where's the (business centre)?
Kur ir (biznesa centrs)?   kur ir (*biz*·ne·sa tsentrs)

I'm attending a ...   *Es piedalos ...*   es *pea*·da·lwas ...
  conference   *konferencē*   kon·fe·ren·tsair
  course   *kursā*   kur·saa
  meeting   *sanāksmē*   sa·*naak*·smair

I'm visiting a trade fair.
Es apmeklēju komercizstādi.   es ap·me·*klair*·yu ko·mer·tsis·taa·di

I have an appointment with ...
Man ir sarunāts tikšanās ar ...   man ir sa·ru·*naats* tik·sha·naas ar ..

I'm with my colleagues.
Es esmu ar kolēģiem.   es *es*·mu ar ko·*lair*·dyeam

Here's my business card.
Šeit ir mana vizītkarte.   shayt ir *ma*·na vi·zeet·kar·te

That went very well.
Tas labi izdevās.   tas *la*·bi iz·de·vaas

emergencies

Help!	*Palīgā!*	pa·lee·gaa
Stop!	*Stāt!*	staat
Go away!	*Ej prom!*	ay prwam
Thief!	*Zaglis!*	zag·lis
Fire!	*Ugunsgrēks!*	u·guns·grairks

Call ...!	*Zvani ...!*	zva·ni ...
an ambulance	*ātrai palīdzībai*	aa·trai pa·lee·dzee·bai
a doctor	*ārstam*	aar·stam
the police	*policijai*	po·li·tsi·yai

Could you help me, please?   *Vai Jūs man varētu palīdzēt, lūdzu?*   vai yoos man *va*·rair·tu pa·lee·dzairt *loo*·dzu

I'm lost.   *Esmu apmaldījies.*   es·mu *ap*·mal·dee·yeas

Where are the toilets?   *Kur ir tualetes?*   kur ir tu·a·le·tes

Latvian

Lithuanian

Breathe in the Baltic coastal scent of mingled ozone and pine in Lithuania.

Pronunciation

Vowels		Consonants	
Symbol	**English sound**	**Symbol**	**English sound**
a	run	b	bed
aa	father	ch	cheat
ai	aisle	d	dog
aw	law	dz	sounds
ay	say	f	fat
e	bet	g	go
ea	ear	h	hat
ee	see	j	joke
ey	as in 'bet', but longer	k	kit
		l	lot
i	hit	m	man
o	pot	n	not
oo	zoo	p	pet
ow	how	r	red (trilled)
u	put	s	sun
wa	water	sh	shot
		t	top
		ts	hats
		v	very
		y	yellow
		z	zero
		zh	pleasure

The Lithuanian pronunciation is given in purple after each word or phrase. Read these words as though you were reading English and you're sure to be understood. Each syllable is separated by a dot, and italics indicate that you need to put stress on that syllable, for example:

Prašau. pra·*show*

Lithuanian

essentials

Yes./No.	*Taip./Ne.*	taip/ne
Hello./Goodbye.	*Sveiki./Viso gero.*	svay·ki/vi·so ge·ro
Please.	*Prašau.*	pra·show
Thank you (very much).	*Ačiū (labai).*	aa·choo (la·bai)
You're welcome.	*Prašom.*	praa·shom
Excuse me.	*Atleiskite.*	at·lays·ki·te
Sorry.	*Atsiprašau.*	at·si·pra·show

Do you speak English?
Ar kalbate angliškai? — ar kal·ba·te aang·lish·kai

Do you understand?
Ar suprantate? — ar su·pran·ta·te

I (don't) understand.
Aš (ne)suprantu. — ash (ne·)su·pran·tu

chatting

introductions

Mr	*Ponas*	paw·nas
Mrs/Ms	*Ponia*	po·nya

How are you?	*Kaip sekasi?*	kaip se·ka·si
Fine. And you?	*Gerai. O kaip jūs?*	ge·rai o kaip yoos
What's your name?	*Koks jūsų vardas?*	kawks yoo·soo var·das
My name is …	*Mano vardas …*	ma·no var·das …
I'm pleased to meet you.	*Malonu susipažinti.*	ma·lo·nu su·si·pa·zhin·ti

Here's my …	*Čia mano …*	chya ma·no …
What's your …?	*Koks jūsų …?*	kawks yoo·soo …
(email) address	*(elektroninio pašto) adresas*	(e·lek·tro·ni·nyo paash·to) aad·re·sas
phone number	*telefono numeris*	te·le·fo·no nu·me·ris

What's your occupation?
Kuo jūs užsiimate? kwa yoos uzh·*si*·i·ma·te

I'm a ...	*Aš esu ...*	ash e·*su* ...
businessperson	*verslininkas* m	*vers*·li·nin·kas
	verslininkė f	*vers*·li·nin·key
student	*studentas* m	stu·*den*·tas
	studentė f	stu·*den*·tey

Where are you from?
Iš kur jūs esate? ish kur yoos e·*sa*·te

I'm from (England).
Aš esu iš (Anglijos). ash e·*su* ish (*aang*·li·yos)

Are you married?
Jūs vedęs/ištekėjusi? m/f yoos ve·des/ish·te·*key*·yu·si

I'm married.
Aš vedęs/ištekėjusi. m/f ash ve·des/ish·te·*key*·yu·si

I'm single.
Aš nevedęs. ash ne·ve·*des*

How old are you?
Kiek jums metų? keak yums *me*·too

I'm ... years old.
Man ... metų. maan ... *me*·too

making conversation

What's the weather like?
Koks dabar oras? kawks da·*bar* aw·ras

It's ...	*Dabar ...*	da·*bar* ...
cold	*šalta*	*shaal*·ta
hot	*karšta*	*kaarsh*·ta
raining	*lyja*	*lee*·ya
snowing	*sninga*	*snin*·ga

Do you live here?
Jūs čia gyvenate? yoos chya *gee*·ve·na·te

Where are you going?
Kur jūs einate? kur yoos *ay*·na·te

What are you doing?
Ką jūs veikiate? kaa yoos *vay*·kya·te

invitations

Would you like to go (for a) ...?	Ar norėtumėte nueiti ...?	ar no·*rey*·tu·mey·te nu·*ay*·ti ...
dancing	*pašokti*	pa·*shawk*·ti
drink	*išgerti*	ish·*ger*·ti
meal	*pavalgyti*	pa·*vaal*·gee·ti
out	*kur nors*	kur nawrs

Yes, I'd love to.
Taip, mielai.   taip *mea*·lai

No, I'm afraid I can't.
Ne, deja, negaliu.   ne de·*ya* ne·ga·*lyu*

I love it here!
Man čia labai patinka!
maan chya la·*bai* pa·*tin*·ka

What time will we meet?
Kada susitinkam?   ka·*da* su·si·*tin*·kam

Where will we meet?
Kur susitinkam?   kur su·si·*tin*·kam

Let's meet at ...	Susitinkam ...	su·si·*tin*·kam ...
(eight) o'clock	*(aštuntą)* *valandą*	(ash·*tun*·taa) vaa·lan·daa
the entrance	*prie įėjimo*	prea ee·ey·*yi*·mo

meeting up

Can I ...?	Ar galiu ...?	ar ga·*lyu* ...
dance with you	*su jumis pašokti*	su yu·*mis* pa·*shawk*·ti
sit here	*čia atsisėsti*	chya at·si·*ses*·ti
take you home	*nuvežti jus namo*	nu·*vezh*·ti yus na·*maw*

I'm here with my girlfriend/boyfriend.
Aš atėjau su savo   ash a·te·*yow* su *saa*·vo
drauge/draugu.   drow·*ge*/drow·*gu*

It's been great meeting you.

Buvo labai malonu bu·vo la·*bai* ma·lo·*nu*
su jumis susipažinti. su yu·*mis* su·si·pa·*zhin*·ti

Keep in touch!

Palaikom ryšį! pa·*lai*·kom ree·shee

likes & dislikes

I thought it	*Man atrodo tai*	man at·*raw*·do tai
was ...	*buvo ...*	*bu*·vo ...
It's ...	*Tai ...*	tai ...
awful	*baisu*	bai·*su*
great	*puiku*	puy·*ku*
interesting	*įdomu*	ee·do·*mu*
Do you like ...?	*Ar jums patinka ...?*	ar yums pa·*tin*·ka ...
I (don't) like ...	*Man (ne)patinka ...*	maan (ne·)pa·*tin*·ka ...
art	*menas*	*me*·nas
shopping	*apsipirkinėti*	ap·si·pir·ki·*ney*·ti
sport	*sportas*	*spor*·tas

eating & drinking

I'd like ..., please.	*Aš norėčiau ...*	ash no·*rey*·chyow ...
a table for	*staliuko*	sta·*lyu*·ko
(four)	*(keturiems)*	(ke·tu·*reams*)
the nonsmoking	*nerūkančių*	ne·*roo*·kan·chyoo
section	*salėje*	*saa*·ley·ye
the smoking	*rūkančių*	*roo*·kan·chyoo
section	*salėje*	*saa*·ley·ye

Do you have vegetarian food?

Ar turite vegetariško maisto? ar tu·ri·te ve·ge·*taa*·rish·ko *mais*·to

What would you recommend?

Ką jūs rekomenduotumėte? kaa yoos re·ko·men·*dwo*·tu·mey·te

I'll have a ...	*Aš užsisakysiu ...*	ash uzh·si·sa·*kee*·syu ...
Cheers!	*Į sveikatą!*	ee svay·*kaa*·taa

I'd like (the) ..., please.	Aš norėčiau ...	ash no·rey·chyow ...
bill	sąskaitos	saas·kai·taws
drink list	gėrimų meniu	gey·ri·moo me·nyu
menu	meniu	me·nyu
that dish	šito patiekalo	shi·to pa·tea·ka·lo

Would you like a drink?
Gal norėtumėte išgerti?
gaal no·rey·tu·mey·te ish·ger·ti

(cup of) coffee/ tea	(puodelio) kavos/ arbatos	(pwa·dey·lyo) ka·vaws/ ar·baa·tos
(mineral) water	(mineralinio) vandens	(mi·ne·raa·li·nyo) van·dens
glass of (wine)	taurės (vyno)	tow·reys (vee·no)
bottle of (beer)	butelio (alaus)	bu·te·lyo (a·lows)

breakfast	pusryčių	pus·ree·chyoo
lunch	lančo	lan·cho
dinner	pietų	pea·too

Lithuanian

exploring

Where's the ...?	Kur yra ...?	kur ee·ra ...
bank	bankas	baan·kas
hotel	viešbutis	veash·bu·tis
post office	paštas	paash·tas

Can you show me (on the map)?
Ar galite parodyti man (žemėlapyje)?   ar gaa·li·te pa·raw·dee·ti maan (zhe·mey·la·pee·ye)

What time does it open/close?
Kada jis atsidaro/užsidaro? m   ka·da yis at·si·daa·ro/uzh·si·da·ro
Kada ji atsidaro/užsidaro? f   ka·da yi at·si·daa·ro/uzh·si·da·ro

What's the admission charge?
Koks įėjimo mokestis?   kawks ee·ey·yi·mo maw·kes·tis

When's the next tour?
Kada bus kita ekskursija?   ka·da bus ki·ta eks·kur·si·ya

Where can I find ...?	*Kur galiu rasti ...?*	kur ga·*lyu* ras·ti ...
clubs	*klubus*	klu·bus
gay venues	*gėjų klubus*	gey·yoo klu·bus
pubs	*barus*	ba·rus

Can we get there by public transport?
Ar galime nuvažiuoti ten   ar ga·li·me nu·va·zhwa·ti ten
viešuoju transportu?   vea·shwa·yu trans·por·tu

Where can I buy a ticket?
Kur galiu nusipirkti bilietą?   kur ga·*lyu* nu·si·*pirk*·ti bi·lye·taa?

One ... ticket (to Kaunas), please.	*Vieną bilietą ... (į Kauną), prašau.*	vea·naa bi·lye·taa ... (ee kow·naa) pra·show
one-way	*į vieną pusę*	ee vea·naa pu·sey
return	*į abi puses*	ee a·bi pu·ses

My luggage has been ...	*Mano bagažas ...*	ma·no ba·gaa·zhas ...
lost	*pasimetė*	pa·si·me·tey
stolen	*buvo pavogtas*	bu·vo pa·vog·tas

Is this the ... to (Klaipėda)?	*Ar čia ... į (Klaipėdą)?*	ar chya ... ee (klai·pey·daa)?
boat	*laivas*	lai·vas
bus	*autobusas*	ow·to·bu·sas
plane	*lėktuvas*	leyk·tu·vas
train	*traukinys*	trow·ki·nees

What time's the ... bus?	*Kada išvažiuoja ... autobusas?*	ka·da ish·va·zhwa·ya ... ow·to·bu·sas
first	*pirmas*	pir·mas
last	*paskutinis*	pas·ku·ti·nis
next	*kitas*	ki·tas

I'd like a taxi ...	*Aš norėčiau taksi ...*	ash no·rey·chyow tak·si ...
at (9am)	*(devintą ryto)*	(de·vin·taa ree·to)
tomorrow	*rytoj*	ree·toy

How much is it to ...?
Kiek kainuos iki ...?   keak kai·nwas i·ki ...

Please take me to (this address).

Prašau nuvežti mane	pra·*show* nu·*vezh*·ti *ma*·ne
(šiuo adresu).	(shi·*wo aad*·re·su)

Please stop here.

Prašau sustoti čia.	pra·*show* su·*sto*·ti chya

shopping

Where's the (market)?	*Kur (turgus)?*	kur (*tur*·gus)
I'm looking for ...	*Aš ieškau ...*	ash *eash*·kow ...
It's faulty.	*Brokuota.*	bro·*kwa*·ta
I'd like ..., please.	*Aš norėčiau ...*	ash no·*rey*·chyow ...
a refund	*atsiimti pinigus*	at·si·*im*·ti *pi*·ni·gus
to return this	*grąžinti*	graa·*zhin*·ti

How much is it?

Kiek kainuoja?	keak kain·*wo*·ya

Can you write down the price?

Ar galite užrašyti kainą?	ar *gaa*·li·te uzh·ra·*shee*·ti *kai*·naa

That's too expensive.

Per brangu.	per *bran*·gu

There's a mistake in the bill.

Sąskaita neteisinga.	*saas*·kai·ta ne·tay·*sin*·ga

I need a film for this camera.

Man reikia juostos šitam	maan *ray*·kya *ywas*·tos shi·*taam*
fotoaparatui.	fo·to·a·pa·*ra*·tuy

Do you accept ...?	*Ar priimate ...?*	ar pri·i·*ma*·te ...
credit cards	*kreditines*	kre·*di*·ti·nes
	korteles	kor·te·*les*
travellers	*kelionės*	ke·*lyo*·nes
cheques	*čekius*	che·*kyus*
I'd like ..., please.	*Norėčiau*	no·*rey*·chyow
	gauti ...	*gow*·ti ...
my change	*savo grąžą*	*sa*·vo *graa*·zhaa
a receipt	*kvitą*	*kvi*·taa

working

Where's the (business centre)?
Kur yra (verslo centras)?   kur ee·ra (vers·lo tsen·tras)

I'm attending a ...   *Aš dalyvauju ...*   ash da·lee·vow·yu ...
    conference   *konferencijoje*   kon·fe·ren·tsi·yo·ye
    course   *kursuose*   kur·swa·se
    meeting   *susitikime*   su·si·ti·ki·me

I'm visiting a trade fair.
Aš atvykau į prekybos mugę.   ash at·vee·kow ee pre·kee·bos mu·gey

I have an appointment with ...
Aš turiu susitikimą su ...   ash tu·ryu su·si·ti·ki·maa su ...

I'm with my colleagues.
Aš čia su savo kolegom.   ash chya su sa·vo ko·le·gom

Here's my business card.
Čia mano vizitinė kortelė.   chya ma·no vi·zi·ti·ney kor·tey·ley

That went very well.
Viskas praėjo labai gerai.   vis·kas pra·ey·yo la·bai ge·rai

emergencies

Help!	*Padėkit!*	pa·dey·kit
Stop!	*Sustokit!*	sus·taw·kit
Go away!	*Eikit iš čia!*	ay·kit ish chya
Thief!	*Vagis!*	va·gis
Fire!	*Ugnis!*	ug·nis
Call ...!	*Iškvieskit ...!*	ish·kveas·kit ...
an ambulance	*greitąją pagalbą*	gray·taa·yaa pa·gal·baa
a doctor	*gydytoją*	gee·dee·to·ya
the police	*policiją*	po·li·tsi·ya
Could you help me, please?	*Gal galėtumėte man padėti?*	gaal ga·ley·tu·mey·te maan pa·dey·ti
I'm lost.	*Aš pasiklydau.*	ash pa·si·klee·dow
Where are the toilets?	*Kur yra tualetai?*	kur ee·ra tu·a·le·tai

Norwegian

Glaciers. Vikings. Walruses. Norway is like
some ancient saga come to life.

Pronunciation

Vowels		Consonants	
Symbol	**English sound**	**Symbol**	**English sound**
a	run	b	bed
aa	father	ch	cheat
ai	aisle	d	dog
aw	saw	f	fat
e	bet	g	go
ee	see	h	hat
eu	nurse	k	kit
ew	ee pronounced with a flared upper lip	l	lot
		m	man
ey	as in 'bet', but longer	n	not
		ng	ring
i	hit	p	pet
o	pot	r	red
oo	soon	s	sun
ow	how	sh	shot
oy	toy	t	top
u	put	v	very
		y	yellow

The Norwegian pronunciation is given in purple after each word or phrase. Read these words as though you were reading English and you're sure to be understood. Each syllable is separated by a dot, and italics indicate that you need to put stress on that syllable, for example:

Unnskyld.   ewn·*shewl*

essentials

Yes./No.	*Ja./Nei.*	yaa/ney
Hello.	*God dag.*	go·daag
Goodbye.	*Ha det.*	haa·de
Please.	*Vær så snill.*	veyr saw snil
Thank you (very much).	*(Tusen) Takk.*	(too·sen) tak
You're welcome.	*Ingen årsak.*	ing·en awr·saak
Excuse me.	*Unnskyld.*	ewn·shewl
Sorry.	*Beklager, tilgi meg.*	bey·klaa·geyr til·yee mai

Do you speak English?
  Snakker du engelsk?   sna·ker doo eyng·elsk

Do you understand?
  Forstår du?   fawr·stawr doo

I (don't) understand.
  Jeg forstår (ikke).   yai fawr·stawr (i·key)

chatting

introductions

Mr	*herr*	heyr
Mrs	*fru*	froo
Miss	*frøken*	freu·ken

How are you?
  Hvordan har du det?   vor·dan haar doo de

Fine. And you?
  Rra. Og du?   braa aw doo

What's your name?
  Hva heter du?   vaa hey·ter doo

My name is ...
  Jeg heter ...   yai hey·ter ...

I'm pleased to meet you.
  Hyggelig å treffe deg.   hew·ge·lee aw tre·fe dai

Norwegian

Here's my ...	Her er min ...	heyr eyr meen ...
What's your ...?	Hva er din ...?	vaa eyr deen ...
(email) address	(e-post)adresse	(ey-post-)a-dre-se
phone number	telefonnummer	te-le-fon-no-mer
What's your occupation?	Hva driver du med?	vaa dree-ver doo mey
I'm a ...	Jeg er ...	yai eyr ...
businessperson	forretnings-drivende	faw-ret-nings-dri-ven-de
student	student	stu-dent

Where are you from?
Hvor er du fra? vor eyr doo fra

I'm from (England).
Jeg er fra (England). yai eyr fraa (eyng-lan)

Are you married?
Er du gift? eyr doo yft

I'm married/single.
Jeg er gift/enslig. yai eyr yft/en-slee

How old are you?
Hvor gammel er du? vor ga-mel eyr doo

I'm ... years old.
Jeg er ... år gammel. yai eyr ... awr ga-mel

making conversation

What's the weather like?
Hvordan er været? vor-dan eyr veyr-re

It's ...		
cold	Det er kaldt.	de eyr kalt
hot	Det er veldig varmt.	de eyr vel-dee varmt
raining	Det regner.	de rai-ner
snowing	Det snør.	de sneur

Do you live here?	Bor du her?	bor doo hayr
Where are you going?	Hvor skal du?	vor skal doo
What are you doing?	Hva gjør du?	vaa yeur doo

96

invitations

Would you like to go (for a) ...?	*Vil du gå ...?*	vil doo gaw ...
dancing	*å danse*	aw *dan*·se
drink	*å ta noe å drikke*	aw taa *naw*·e aw *dri*·ke
meal	*å spise*	aw *spee*·se
out	*ut*	oot

Yes, I'd love to.
Ja, det vil jeg gjerne.   ya de vil yai *yer*·ne

No, I'm afraid I can't.
Beklager, jeg kan ikke.   bey·*klaa*·geyr yai kan *i*·key

I love it here!
Det er kjempefint her!
de eyr chem·pe·*feent* heyr

What time will we meet?
Når skal vi møtes?   naar skal vee *meu*·tes

Where will we meet?
Hvor skal vi møtes?   vor skal vee *meu*·tes

Let's meet at ...	*Vi møtes ...*	vee *meu*·tes ...
(eight) o'clock	*klokken (åtte)*	*klaw*·ka (*aw*·te)
the entrance	*ved inngangen*	ve *in*·gang·en

meeting up

Can I ...?	*Kan jeg ...?*	kan yai ...
dance with you	*få en dans*	faw en dans
sit here	*sitte her*	*si*·te heyr
take you home	*følge deg hjem*	*feul*·ge dai yem

I'm here with my girlfriend/boyfriend.
Jeg er her med   yai er heyr mey
kjæresten min.   *shey*·re·sten meen

It's been great meeting you.
Det var morsomt   de vaar *mawr*·somt
å treffe deg.   aw *tre*·fe dai

Keep in touch!
Hold kontakten!   hawl kon·*tak*·ten

likes & dislikes

I thought it was ...	Jeg syntes det var ...	yai *su*·nes de var ...
It's ...	Det er ...	de eyr ...
awful	forferdelig	fawr·*fer*·de·lee
great	kjempefint	chem·pe·*feent*
interesting	interessant	in·tre·*sant*
Do you like ...?	Liker du ...?	*lee*·ker doo ...
I (don't) like ...	Jeg liker (ikke) ...	yai *lee*·ker (*i*·key) ...
art	kunst	koonst
shopping	å handle	aw *hand*·le
sport	sport	spawrt

eating & drinking

I'd like ..., please.	Jeg vil gjerne ha ..., takk.	yai vil *yer*·ne ha ... tak
the nonsmoking section	på ikke-røyke	paw *i*·key·*roy*·ke
the smoking section	der man kan røyke	deyr man kan *roy*·ke
a table for (four)	et bord til (fire)	et bawr til (*fee*·re)

Do you have vegetarian food?
Har du vegetariansk   har doo ve·ge·ta·ree·*ansk*
mat her?   maat heyr

What would you recommend?
Hva vil du anbefale?   va vil doo *an*·be·fa·le

I'll have a ...	Jeg vil ha ...	yai vil haa ...
Cheers!	Skål!	skawl

I'd like (the) …, please.	Kan jeg få …, takk.	kan yai faw … tak
bill	regningen	rai·ning·en
drink list	vinlisten	veen·lis·ten
menu	menyen	me·new·en
that dish	den retten	den re·ten

Would you like a drink?
Vil du ha noe å drikke?
vil doo haa *naw*·e aw *dri*·ke

(cup of) coffee/tea	(en kopp) kaffe/te	(en kawp) *kaa*·fe/te
(mineral) water	(mineral)vann	(mi·ne·*ral*·)van
bottle of (beer)	en flaske (øl)	en *flas*·ke (eul)
glass of (wine)	et glass (vin)	et glas (veen)
breakfast	frokost	*fro*·kost
lunch	lunsj	loonsh
dinner	middag	*mi*·da

exploring

Where's the …?	Hvor er …?	vor eyr …
bank	banken	*ban*·ken
hotel	hotellet	hoo·*te*·ley
post office	postkontoret	*pawst*·kawn·taw·rey

Can you show me (on the map)?
Kan du vise meg
(på kartet)?
kan doo *vee*·sey mai
(paw *kar*·te)

What time does it open/close?
Når åpner/stenger det?
nawr *awp*·ner/*steng*·er de

What's the admission charge?
Hvor mye koster det
å komme inn?
vor *mew*·e *kos*·ter de
aw *kaw*·me in

When's the next tour?
Når går neste tur?
nawr gawr *nes*·te toor

99

Where can I find ...? *Hvor er det ...?* vor eyr de ...
clubs *klubber* *kloo*·ber
gay venues *homseklubber* *hom*·se·*kloo*·ber
pubs *barer* *ba*·rer

Can we get there by public transport?
Kan vi dra dit med offentlig kan vee dra deet mey of·ent·lee
transport? tran·*sport*

Where can I buy a ticket?
Hvor kan jeg kjøpe billett? vor kan yai *sheu*·pe bee·*let*

One ... ticket *Jeg vil gjerne ha ...* yai vil *yer*·ne haa ...
(to Bergen), please. *(til Bergen), takk.* (til *ber*·gen) tak
one-way *enveisbillett* en·*veys*·bee·*let*
return *returbillett* re·*toor*·bi·*let*

My luggage has *Bagasjen min* ba·*gaa*·shen meen
been ... *er ...* eyr ...
lost *blitt borte* blit *bawr*·te
stolen *stjålet* *styaw*·let

Is this the ... *Er dette ...* er de·*tey* ...
to (Oslo)? *til (Oslo)?* til (*os*·law)
boat *båten* *baw*·ten
bus *bussen* *bu*·sen
plane *flyet* *flew*·e
train *toget* *taw*·ge

What time's *Når går ... buss?* nawr gawr ... bus
the ... bus?
first *første* *feur*·ste
last *siste* *si*·ste
next *neste* *ne*·ste

I'd like a taxi ... *Jeg vil gjerne ha* yai vil *yer*·ne haa
en drosje ... en *draw*·shey ...
at (9am) *klokka (ni* *klaw*·ka (nee
om morgenen) awm *mawr*·ge·nen)
tomorrow *i morgen* ee *maw*·ren

How much is it to ...?
Hvor mye koster det vor *mew*·e *kaws*·ter de
å kjøre til ...? aw *sheu*·re til ...

Please take me to (this address).
*Kan du kjøre meg til
(denne adressen)?*
kan doo *sheu*·re mai til
(*dey*·ne a·*dre*·sen)

Please stop here.
Vær så snill å stoppe her.
veyr saw snil aw *sto*·pe heyr

shopping

Where's the (market)?	*Hvor er det (marked)?*	vor eyr de (*mar*·ked)
I'm looking for ...	*Jeg leter etter ...*	yai *ley*·ter e·ter ...
It's faulty.	*Den er ødelagt.*	den eyr *eud*·lagt
I'd like ..., please.	*Jeg vil gjerne ..., takk.*	yai vil *yer*·ne ... tak
a refund	*ha refusjon*	haa re·foo·*shawn*
to return this	*returnere dette*	re·*toor*·ne·re *dey*·te

How much is it?
Hvor mye koster det?
vor *mew*·e *kaws*·ter de

Can you write down the price?
Kan du skrive ned prisen?
kan doo *skree*·ve ned *pree*·sen

That's too expensive.
Det er for dyrt.
de eyr fawr dewrt

There's a mistake in the bill.
Det er en feil på regningen.
de eyr en fail paw *rai*·ning·en

I need a film for this camera.
*Jeg vil gjerne ha ...
film til dette kameraet.*
yai vil *yer*·ne haa ...
film til *dey*·te *ka*·me·raa

Do you accept ...?	*Tar du imot ...?*	taar doo ee·*mot*
credit cards	*kredittkort*	kre·*dit*·kawrt
travellers cheques	*reisesjekker*	*rai*·se·*shey*·ker

I'd like ..., please.	*Jeg vil gjerne ha igjen ..., takk.*	yai vil *yer*·ne haa ee·*yen* ... tak
a receipt	*kvittering*	kvee·*te*·ring
my change	*vekslepenger*	*vek*·sle·*peyng*·er

working

I'm attending a ...	Jeg er på ...	yai ayr paw ...
conference	en konferanse	en kawn·fe·ran·se
course	et kurs	et kurs
meeting	et møte	meu·te

Where's the (business centre)?
Hvor er (sentrum)? vor ayr (sen·trum)

I'm visiting a trade fair.
Jeg er på en varemesse. yai ayr paw en va·re·me·se

I have an appointment with ...
Jeg har et møte med ... yai har et meu·te me ...

I'm with my colleagues.
Jeg er sammen med kollegaer. yai er sa·men me ko·le·ger

Here's my business card.
Her er visittkortet mitt. hayr ayr vi·sit·kor·te meet

That went very well.
Det gikk veldig bra. de yeek vel·di bra

emergencies

Help!	Hjelp!	yelp
Stop!	Stopp!	stawp
Go away!	Forsvinn!	fawr·svin
Thief!	Tyv!	teev
Fire!	Brann!	bran

Call ...!	Ring ...!	ring ...
an ambulance	etter sykebil	e·ter sew·ke·bil
a doctor	en lege	en le·ge
the police	politiet	po·lee·tee·ay

Could you help me, please?
Kan du være så snill å hjelpe meg? kan doo vey·re saw snil aw yel·pe mai

I'm lost.
Jeg har gått meg vill. yai har gawt mai vil

Where are the toilets?
Hvor er toalettene? vor eyr to·aa·le·te·ne

Swedish

The dream of a blond populace enjoying a fabulously high standard of living is not too far from the truth.

Pronunciation

Vowels		Consonants	
Symbol	English sound	Symbol	English sound
a	run	b	bed
aa	father	ch	cheat
ai	aisle	d	dog
aw	saw	f	fat
e	bet	fh	f pronounced with rounded lips
air	hair		
ee	see	g	go
eu	nurse	h	hat
ew	ee pronounced with rounded lips	k	kit
		l	lot
ey	as in 'bet', but longer	m	man
		n	not
i	hit	ng	ring
o	pot	p	pet
oh	oh	r	red
oo	zoo	s	sun
u	put	sh	shot
		t	top
		v	very
		y	yes

The Swedish pronunciation is given in purple after each word or phrase. Read these words as though you were reading English and you're sure to be understood. Each syllable is separated by a dot, and italics indicate that you need to put stress on that syllable, for example:

Ursäkta mig.   oor·*shek*·ta mey

Swedish

essentials

Yes./No.	*Ja./Nej.*	yaa/ney
Hello./Goodbye.	*Hej./Adjö.*	hey/aa·*yeu*
Please.	*Tack.*	tak
Thank you (very much).	*Tack (så mycket).*	tak (saw *mew*·ke)
You're welcome.	*Varsågod.*	var·sha·*gohd*
Excuse me.	*Ursäkta mig.*	oor·*shek*·ta mey
Sorry.	*Förlåt.*	feur·*lawt*

Do you speak English?
  Talar du engelska?   taa·lar doo eng·el·ska

Do you understand?
  Förstår du?   feur·*shtawr* doo

I (don't) understand.
  Jag förstår (inte).   yaa feur·*shtawr* (*in*·te)

chatting

introductions

Mr	*herr*	her
Mrs	*fru*	froo
Miss	*fröken*	*freu*·ken

How are you?	*Hur står det till?*	hoor stawr de til
Fine. And you?	*Bra. Och dig?*	braa o dey
What's your name?	*Vad heter du?*	vaad *hey*·ter doo
My name is ...	*Jag heter ...*	yaa *hey*·ter ...
I'm pleased to meet you.	*Trevligt att träffas.*	*treyv*·lit at *tre*·fas

Here's my (email) address.
  Här är min (e-post) adress.   hair air min (*ey*·post) a·*dres*

What's your (email) address?
  Vad är din (e-post) adress?   vaad air din (*ey*·post) a·*dres*

105

Here's my phone number.
Här är mitt telefonnummer.   hair air mit te·le·*fohn*·nu·mer

What's your phone number?
Vad är ditt telefonnummer?   vaad air dit te·le·*fohn*·nu·mer

What's your occupation?
Vad har du för yrke?   vaad har doo feur *ewr*·ke

I'm a ...   *Jag är ...*   yaa air ...
     businessperson   *affärsman*   a·*fairsh*·man
     student   *studerande*   stu·*dey*·ran·de

Where are you from?
Varifrån kommer du?   var·ee·frawn *ko*·mer doo

I'm from (England).
Jag kommer från (England).   yaa *ko*·mer frawn (*eng*·land)

Are you married?
Är du gift?   air doo yift

I'm married/single.
Jag är gift/ogift.   yaa air yift/*oh*·yift

How old are you?
Hur gammal är du?   hoor *ga*·mal air doo

I'm ... years old.
Jag är ... år gammal.   yaa air ... awr *ga*·mal

making conversation

What's the weather like?
Hur är vädret?   hur air *vey*·dret

It's...
cold	*Det är kallt.*	de air kalt
hot	*Det är hett.*	de air het
raining	*Det regnar.*	de *reng*·nar
snowing	*Det snöar.*	de *sneu*·ar

Do you live here?	*Bor du här?*	bor doo hair
Where are you going?	*Vart går du?*	vaart gawr doo
What are you doing?	*Vad gör du?*	vaad yeur doo

invitations

Would you like to go (for a) ...?	*Vill du gå ut ...?*	vil doo gaw oot ...
dancing	*och dansa*	o *dan*·sa
drink	*och ta en drink*	o taa eyn drink
meal	*och äta*	o *air*·ta
out somewhere	*någonstans*	*nawn*·stans

Yes, I'd love to.
Ja, gärna. yaa *yair*·na

No, I'm afraid I can't.
Nej, tyvärr kan jag inte. ney tew·*vair* kan yaa *in*·te

I love it here!
Jag gillar att vara här!
yaa *yi*·lar at *vaa*·ra hair

What time will we meet?
Hur dags ska vi träffas? hoor daks ska vee *tre*·fas

Where will we meet?
Var ska vi träffas? var ska vee *tre*·fas

Let's meet at ...	*Ska vi träffas ...?*	ska vee *tre*·fas ...
(eight) o'clock	*klockan (åtta)*	*klo*·kan (*aw*·ta)
the entrance	*vid ingången*	veed *in*·gawng·en

meeting up

Can I ...?	*Får jag ...?*	fawr yaa ...
dance with you	*dansa med dig*	*dan*·sa mey dey
sit here	*sitta här*	*si*·ta hair
take you home	*ta dig hem*	taa dey hem

I'm here with my girlfriend/boyfriend.
Jag är här med min yaa air hair meyd min
flickvän/pojkvän. flik·ven/*poyk*·ven

It's been great meeting you.
Trevligt att träffas.   trey·vlit at tre·fas

Keep in touch!
Hör av dig!   heur aav dey

likes & dislikes

I thought it was ...	*Jag tyckte att det var ...*	yaa *tewk*·te at de var ...
It's ...	*Det är ...*	de air ...
awful	*hemskt*	hemskt
great	*utmärkt*	*oot*·mairkt
interesting	*interessant*	in·te·re·*sant*
Do you like ...?	*Tycker du om ...?*	*tew*·ker doo om ...
I (don't) like ...	*Jag tycker (inte) om ...*	yaa *tew*·ker (*in*·te) om ...
art	*konst*	konst
shopping	*att shoppa*	at *sho*·pa
sport	*sport*	sport

eating & drinking

I'd like ..., please.	*... , tack.*	... tak
the nonsmoking section	*Rökfria avdelningen*	*reuk*·free·a *aav*·del·ning·en
the smoking section	*Rökavdelningen*	*reuk*·aav·del·ning·en
a table for (four)	*Ett bord för (fyra)*	et bord feur (*few*·ra)

Do you have vegetarian food?
Har ni vegetarisk mat?   har nee ve·ge·*taa*·risk maat

What would you recommend?
Vad skulle ni anbefalla?   vaad *sku*·le nee *an*·be·fa·la

I'll have a ...	*Jag vill ha ...*	yaa vil haa ...
Cheers!	*Skål!*	skawl

I'd like (the) …, please.	Jag skulle vilja ha …	yaa *sku*·le *vil*·ya haa …
bill	räkningen	*reyk*·ning·en
drink list	d"drickslistan	*driks*·lis·tan
menu	menyn	me·*newn*
that dish	den maträtt	deyn maat·ret

Would you like a drink?
Vill du ha en drink?
vil doo haa eyn drink

(cup of) coffee/tea	(en kopp) kaffe/te	(eyn kop) *ka*·fe/tey
(mineral) water	(mineral)vatten	(mi·ne·*raal*·)va·ten
bottle of (beer)	en flaska (öl)	eyn *flas*·ka (eul)
glass of (wine)	ett glas (vin)	et glaas (veen)
breakfast	frukost	*froo*·kost
lunch	lunch	lunsh
dinner	middag	*mi*·daa

Swedish

exploring

Where's the …?	Var ligger …?	var *li*·ger …
bank	banken	*ban*·ken
hotel	hotellet	hoh·*te*·let
post office	posten	*pos*·ten

Can you show me (on the map)?
Kan du visa mig (på kartan)?
kan doo *vee*·sa mey (paw *kar*·tan)

What time does it open/close?
Hur dags öppnar/stänger de?
hoor daks *eup*·nar/*steng*·ar dom

What's the admission charge?
Hur mycket kostar det i inträde?
hoor *mew*·ke *kos*·tar de i *in*·trey·de

When's the next tour?
När avgår nästa turen?
nair *aav*·gawr *nes*·ta *too*·ren

Where can I find ...?	*Var finns ...?*	var fins ...
clubs	*klubbarna*	*klu·bar·na*
gay venues	*gayklubbarna*	*gay·klu·bar·na*
pubs	*pubbarna*	*pu·bar·na*

Can we get there by public transport?
Kan vi åka dit med   kan vee *aw·*ka deet meyd
lokaltrafik?   loh·*kaal·*tra·*feek*

Where can I buy a ticket?
Var kan jag köpa en biljett?   var kan yaa *sheu·*pa eyn bil·*yet*

One ... ticket (to Stockholm), please.	*Jag skulle vilja ha en ... (till Stockholm).*	yaa *sku·*le *vil·*ya haa eyn ... (til *stok·*holm)
one-way	*enkelbiljett*	*en·*kel·bil·*yet*
return	*returbiljett*	re·*toor·*bil·*yet*

My luggage has been ...	*Mit bagage är blivit ...*	mit ba·*gaash* air *blee·*vit ...
lost	*förlorat*	feur·*loh·*rat
stolen	*stulit*	*stoo·*lit

Is this the ... to (Stockholm)?	*Är den här ... till (Stockholm)?*	air den hair ... til (*stok·*holm)
boat	*båten*	*baw·*ten
bus	*bussen*	*bu·*sen

Is this the ... to (Stockholm)?	*Är det här ... till (Stockholm)?*	air de hair ... til (*stok·*holm)
plane	*planet*	*plaa·*net
train	*tåget*	*taw·*get

What time's the ... bus?	*När går ...?*	nair gawr ...
first	*första bussen*	*feursh·*ta *bu·*sen
last	*sista bussen*	*sis·*ta *bu·*sen
next	*nästa buss*	*nes·*ta bus

I'd like a taxi ...	*Jag vill gärna få en taxi ...*	yaa vil *yair·*na faw eyn *tak·*see ...
at (9am)	*klockan (nio på morgonen)*	*klo·*kan (*nee·*oh paw *mo·*ro·nen)
tomorrow	*imorgon*	ee·*mo·*ron

How much is it to …?
Vad kostar det till …?   vaad *kos*·tar de til …

Please take me to (this address).
Kan du köra mig till   kan doo *sheu*·ra mey til
(denna address)?   (*dey*·na a·*dres*)

Please stop here.
Kan du stanna här?   kan doo *sta*·na hair

shopping

Where's the (market)?	*Var ligger (salutorget)?*	var *li*·ger (saa·loo·*tor*·yet)
I'm looking for …	*Jag letar efter …*	yaa *ley*·tar *ef*·ter …
It's faulty.	*Den är felaktig.*	deyn air *fey*·lak·ti
I'd like …, please.	*Jag vill gärna …*	yaa vil *yair*·na …
a refund	*få en återbäring*	faw eyn *aw*·ter·bai·ring
to return this	*återlämna denna*	*aw*·ter·lem·na *dey*·na

How much is it?
Hur mycket kostar det?   hoor *mew*·ke *kos*·tar de

Can you write down the price?
Kan du skriva ner priset?   kan du *skree*·va neyr *pree*·set

That's too expensive.
Det är för dyrt.   de air feur dewrt

There's a mistake in the bill.
Det är ett fel på räkningen.   de air et fel paw *reyk*·ning·en

I need a film for this camera.
Jag skulle vilja ha en film   yaa *sku*·le *vil*·ya haa eyn film
till den här kameran.   til deyn hair *kaa*·me·ra

Do you accept …?	*Tar ni …?*	tar nee …
credit cards	*kreditkort*	kre·*deet*·kort
travellers cheques	*resecheckar*	*rey*·se·she·kar
I'd like …, please.	*Jag vill gärna ha …*	yaa vil *yair*·na ha …
a receipt	*ett kvitto*	et *kvi*·to
my change	*min växel*	min *vek*·sel

Swedish

111

working

Where's the (business centre)?
Var är (affärsecentret)?   var air (a·*fairsh*·sent·tret)

I'm attending a ...   *Jag deltar i ...*   yaa *del*·tar ee ...
  conference   *konferens*   kon·fe·*rens*
  course   *en kurs*   en koosh
  meeting   *ett möte*   et *meu*·te

I'm visiting a trade fair.
Jag går på handelsmässa.   yaa gawr paw han·dels·*me*·sa

I have an appointment with ...
Jag har en tidsbeställning med ...   yaa har eyn *teeds*·be·stel·ning mey ...

I'm with my colleagues.
Jag är här med mina kollegor.   yaa air hair mey *mee*·na ko·*ley*·gor

Here's my business card.
Här är mitt affärskort.   hair air mit a·*fairsh*·kort

That went very well.
Det gick mycket bra.   dey yik *mew*·ke braa

emergencies

Help!   *Hjälp!*   yelp
Stop!   *Stanna!*   *sta*·na
Go away!   *Försvinn!*   feur·*shvin*
Thief!   *Ta fast tjuven!*   ta fast *shoo*·ven
Fire!   *Elden är lös!*   *el*·den air leus

Call ...!   *Ring ...!*   ring ...
  an ambulance   *efter en ambulans*   *ef*·ter en am·boo·*lans*
  a doctor   *efter en doktor*   *ef*·ter en *dok*·tor
  the police   *polisen*   poh·*lee*·sen

Could you help me, please?   *Kan du hjälpa mig?*   kan doo *yel*·pa mai
I'm lost.   *Jag har gått vilse.*   yaa har got *vil*·se
Where are the toilets?   *Var är toaletten?*   var air toh·aa·*le*·ten

Swedish

24 hours in the city

Enjoying a city break? Hit the streets and savour every second ...

Copenhagen

9am Start in Strøget, Copenhagen's famous pedestrian street, with a coffee and a *wienerbrød* (Danish pastry) in any of the numerous cafés. Check out the action in City Hall Square on your way to the Dansk Design Center to see some seriously innovative Danish design.

1pm After a quick trip to Tivoli Gardens, head to Ida Davidsen for a lunch of *smørrebrød* (open sandwiches) and fjord prawns – you'll melt in front of the 250-strong selection of sandwiches.

3pm Walk across Knippelsbro, a wonderful Funkis-style bridge, to the island of Christianshavn, where you can hire a boat and explore this delightful locale's historic canals. Later, enjoy a *fadøl* (draught beer) at an outdoor table at Nyhavn, followed by dinner at Restaurant Leonora Christine in Nyhavn's oldest building.

7pm Catch the Danish Royal Ballet at the Det Kongelige Teater (Royal Theatre) and end your night by sampling a few cocktails at retro-style Barbarella, open until very late – or is that very early?

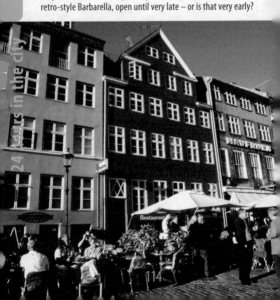

Helsinki

8am Begin with a strong coffee at the Strindberg with a cardamom-flavoured *pulla* (sweet bread ring), then take the short stroll to the harbour-side *kauppatori* (market square) in search of salmon chowder.

11am Ferry yourself (and your picnic) to historic Suomenlinna Island, the 'fortress of Finland'. Back on the mainland, hie yourself to rock-hewn Temppeliaukio Church and listen to gospel in its fantastic acoustics.

3pm Check out the imposing 19th-century Senate Square and take in the scene from the steps of the blue-domed Lutheran Chapel, then, in the interests of religious balance, roam through the Uspenski Orthodox Cathedral. Browse through the Atheneum gallery for some classic art from the Finnish golden age.

6pm Time for sweating, dining and drinking. Try a sauna at Kotiharjun Sauna, a meal at the Boathouse restaurant on an island in Helsinki harbour, and a night at legendary rock venue Tavastia.

Nuuk

7.30am Get out there on the fjords — early morning is the perfect time for fishing. Bag your catch to bring it back, then go for a community breakfast or *kaffemik* (coffee and, usually, seven types of cakes or biscuits).

11am Head to Braedet Market, where fresh fish and game are sold on open-air tables, and roam through Kolonihavn — an 18th-century fishing village nestled in the heart of Nuuk.

3pm Check out ancient and modern Inuit art at the Katuaq Cultural Centre, or if you're there at the right time of year, watch snow-sculptors at work at the annual Nuuk International Snow Festival.

7pm Dinner can only be gourmet Arctic gastronomy (like musk steak) at Restaurant Nipisa.

9pm Drink up in Kristinemut, Greenland's first pub, then party on in the electro-throbbing rock bar Afterdark. You may get lucky enough to see Nuuk Posse, Greenland's most popular hip-hop band, perform.

24 hours in the city

Oslo

9am Poke around in the Akerhus Festning, the earthen-walled palace offering excellent views of the city and Oslofjord.

11am Take a ferry to the Vikingskiphuset (Viking ship museum) to check out the excavated burial ships built in the 9th century, then marvel at the 18th-century buildings of the Norsk Folkemuseum.

1.30pm Return to town to enjoy an espresso under the beautiful ceiling of Tekehtopa. Later, wander through Vigelan Park, the central walkway of Oslo's Frognerparken.

4pm Browse the boutiques of the Grünerløkka district and seat yourself at the pavement café of Parkteateret for a beer while overlooking one of the area's English squares.

8pm Dine at Frognerseteren – make sure you don't miss the mountaintop apple cake for dessert. Follow it up with an evening at the Blå cultural centre, either indoors for the jazz or outside overlooking the river.

Reykjavík

10am Belly-flop yourself awake in the Luagadalur thermal pool, blocking out memories of the night before, then browse the Kolaportið flea markets.

1pm Grab the obligatory Reykjavík lunch of hot dog with *remúladi* (mayonnaise sauce) and crispy-fried onion from Bœjarins Bestu before heading off to an opening of a contemporary sculpture exhibition at Hafnarhúsið.

4pm Settle in for chess at Grand Rokk bar with the Hrokurinn Chess Club when it's too cold to horse-ride or hike.

7.30pm Head to Siggi Hall's eponymous restaurant. Puffin pies are among the mains, but don't miss the *skyr* dessert – a yogurt-like concoction paired with lush local berries.

9pm Your best Friday night option is unquestionably drinking copious amounts of vodka-spiked beer with the *runtur* (literally 'round tour') crowd around Laugavegur in the town centre – the ultimate pub-crawl.

Rīga

9am Start your day in Vecrīga (Old Rīga), the city's historical heart with a skyline dominated by three steeples: St Peter's, the Dome Cathedral and St Jacob's. Breakfast among the colourful houses and the Art Nouveau architectural creations.

12.30pm Pass through Rīga's central market and snaffle yourself some exquisite amber, then cross one of the city's three bridges to reach the more modern left bank. You won't be left cold by the contemporary cool on this side of the river.

3pm Dash off to the seaside resort of Jūrmala to make the most of the near-Arctic summer.

7pm After dark head back to Vecrīga, the hub of sleek restaurants and cool bars. Dine on garlic-anything (yes, including desserts) at Kiploka Krogs.

9pm Don't miss the productions put on at the National Opera House and dare to try some lethal Rīga Black Balsam for your after-opera drinks.

Stockholm

8am Have a *lussekatt* (saffron bun) and coffee at Thelins Konditori in Kungsholmen. Make your way to Skeppsholmen to view the Moderna Museet's world-class collection of modern art, sculpture and installations.

11am Hop on the *tunnelbana* (metro) to Gamla Stan in time to watch the midday changing of the guards at Kungliga Slottet (the Royal Palace). Wander the cobbled streets of the old town, stopping to *fika* (have coffee and cake) in the city's oldest café, Sundbergs Konditori.

3pm Take in the 'time-travel' exhibit of Stockholm's growth and culture at Stockholms Stadsmuseum. Then catch the Katarinahissen lift to the top of the bridge and enjoy the spectacular evening view.

7pm Dine at Eriks Gondolen atop Katrinahissen or try the *husmanskost* (traditional Swedish fare) at Östgötakällaren. Afterwards, join enthusiastic locals at one of the bars in Södermalm, Stockholm's undisputed capital of alcohol consumption.

24 hours in the city

Tallinn

7.30am Start early to avoid the cruise-ship crowds. Breakfast in Raekoja Plats at a street-side café and take a stroll through the Old Town watching shop owners setting up for the day. Do your Upper and Lower Town sightseeing now.

11am Walk east along busy Narva maantee and get a flavour of Tallinn's newish downtown hustle and bustle. Head to the romantic Gloria Veinikelder restaurant (which once hosted Soviet canoodlers from St Petersburg) for lunch.

3pm Check out the suburb of Kradriorg, eye off the Palace of Peter the Great and don't miss out on its Museum of Foreign Art. Dash off to Pirita and the seaside road – try a mid-afternoon coffee and cake while you bathe in the sunset light.

7pm After a vigorous rubdown at the Kalamaja sauna, sneak around Kalamaja's backstreets and try some of Tallinn's cheapest shots. Take in experimental theatre at the Von Krahli Theatre and see the night out in the Old Town.

Tórshavn

8am Begin with breakfast harbour-side in the atmospheric Karlsborg Café, then observe Tórshavn from the sea in one of the two antique wooden sloops moored in the harbour.

1pm Gorge yourself on the lunch buffet at the Marco Polo to celebrate your sail and wander through the city's historical core of Tinganes. Take in the view from the lighthouse located at Skansin Fort.

4pm Get out of town for the afternoon to Føroya Fornminnisavn (Historical Museum) – don't miss the Faroese artefacts from the Viking Age on the main site, and the gorgeous 1920s farmhouse on the second site. If you still have some time, try the Listasavn Føroya (National Art Gallery) for classic and contemporary art.

8pm Sample the seafood buffet at Restaurant Hafnia, then savour a cabaret performance at Leikhúsið Gríma. End the night at the Gallaria Jinx to check out the art and hang out with the hippest folk in the Faroes.

24 hours in the city

Vilnius

9am Start by roaming the *senamiestis* (cobbled streets) of the World Heritage–listed Old Town. Signs are in English and Lithuanian, so no excuses for not trying!

11am Cruise the blue lagoon around Trakai Castle in a yacht and check out the battlements from water level. Back on land, head to the craft markets of Pilies gatvė for the perfect souvenir.

3pm See the treasure-trove of religious works on display at the Museum of Applied Arts, then work off all that culture with a hike up Gediminas Hill for a sublime sunset over the city spires.

6pm For dinner, sample smoked pig's ears at Rotis Smuklè while the spit roast turns, and move on to Mano Kavinè, a funky studenty hang-out, to try a 'Neprisikashkopustelaujancho punch'. (How many drinks will you need to be able to pronounce it right?)

9pm For your night-time explorations head to Bix, formed by the Lithuanian hard-rock band of the same name – its avant-garde industrial décor makes it a favourite among the city's youngsters.

Index

Index

	Dan	Est	Far	Fin	Gre	Ice	Lat	Lit	Nor	Swe
S										
shopping	21	31	41	51	61	71	81	91	101	111
sightseeing	19	29	39	49	59	69	79	89	99	109
sport	18	28	38	48	58	68	78	88	98	108
Stockholm						120				
T										
Talinn						121				
taxi	20	30	40	50	60	70	80	90	100	110
telephone	16	25	35	45	55	66	75	85	96	106
tickets	20	30	40	50	60	70	50	90	100	110
titles	15	25	35	45	–	65	75	85	95	105
toilets	22	32	42	52	662	72	82	92	102	112
Tórshavn						122				
tours	19	29	39	49	59	69	79	89	99	109
trade fair	22	32	42	52	62	72	82	92	102	112
train	20	30	–	50	–	–	80	90	100	110
travellers cheques	21	31	41	51	61	71	81	91	101	111
V										
vegetarian food	18	28	38	48	58	68	78	88	98	108
Vilnius						123				
W										
weather	16	26	36	46	56	66	76	86	96	106
working	22	32	42	52	62	72	82	92	102	112

Index

Internal photographs: p114 Nyhavn restaurants, Copenhagen – John Elk III • p115 Lutheran Cathedral, Helsinki – Adrian Beesley/iStockphoto • p116 Statue of Kassassuak, Nuuk – Anders Blomqvist • p117 Royal Palace, Oslo – iStockphoto • p118 Sun-Craft sculpture, Reykjavík – Anders Blomqvist • p119 Local youth in Town Hall Square, Riga – Bruce Yuanyue Bi • p120 Gold crown in front of the Old Town, Stockholm – Wayne Walton • p121 Wind vane in the centre of historic Tallinn – Samuli Siltanen/iStockphoto • p122 Harbour of Tórshavn – iStockphoto • p123 Local youth in Cathedral Square, Vilnius – Bruce Yuanyue Bi

What kind of traveller are you?

A. You're eating chicken for dinner *again* because it's the only word you know.

B. When no one understands what you say, you step closer and shout louder.

C. When the barman doesn't understand your order, you point frantically at the beer.

D. You're surrounded by locals, swapping jokes, email addresses and experiences – other travellers want to borrow your phrasebook or audio guide.

If you answered A, B, or C, you NEED Lonely Planet's language products ...

- **Lonely Planet Phrasebooks** – for every phrase you need in every language you want
- **Lonely Planet Language & Culture** – get behind the scenes of English as it's spoken around the world – learn and laugh
- **Lonely Planet Fast Talk & Fast Talk Audio** – essential phrases for short trips and weekends away – read, listen and talk like a local
- **Lonely Planet Small Talk** – 10 essential languages for city breaks
- **Lonely Planet Real Talk** – downloadable language audio guides from lonelyplanet.com to your MP3 player

... and this is why

- **Talk to everyone everywhere**
  Over 120 languages, more than any other publisher
- **The right words at the right time**
  Quick-reference colour sections, two-way dictionary, easy pronunciation, every possible subject – and audio to support it

Lonely Planet Offices

Australia	**USA**	**UK**
90 Maribyrnong St, Footscray,	150 Linden St, Oakland,	2nd floor, 186 City Rd,
Victoria 3011	CA 94607	London EC1V 2NT
☎ 03 8379 8000	☎ 510 893 8555	☎ 020 7106 2100
fax 03 8379 8111	fax 510 893 8572	fax 020 7106 2101
✉ talk2us@lonelyplanet.com.au	✉ info@lonelyplanet.com	✉ go@lonelyplanet.co.uk

lonelyplanet.com